Building Up the Kingdom, One Bible Talk at a Time

By

William Peña

Building Up the Kingdom, One Bible Talk at a Time

Table of Contents

Introduction

They devoted themselves to the apostles' teaching and to fellowship, to the breaking of bread and to prayer. Everyone was filled with awe at the many wonders and signs performed by the apostles. All the believers were together and had everything in common. They sold property and possessions to give to anyone who had need. Every day they continued to meet together in the temple courts. They broke bread in their homes and ate together with glad and sincere hearts, praising God and enjoying the favor of all the people. And the Lord added to their number daily those who were being saved.

—Acts 2:42-47 NIV

From the beginning of creation, God's greatest desire has been to have a family—a people who love Him wholeheartedly and keep Him at the center of their lives.

Though Adam, Eve, and even the Israelites fell short of fulfilling this dream, God's determination never wavered. His vision for

His kingdom remained: a family on Earth where He would reign as King, leading through His Word and lavishing His love on His people.

THE CHURCH IS BORN

On the Day of Pentecost, God fulfilled His promise in a powerful way. The Holy Spirit descended upon the apostles, equipping them to declare the arrival of His long-awaited kingdom.

Through miraculous signs and wonders, they announced that the time had come for God to gather His family. Peter extended an invitation that was both simple and profound: turn from sin, make Jesus Lord, be baptized for the forgiveness of sins, and receive the gift of the Holy Spirit.

That day, 3,000 people embraced this life-changing call and became the first members of God's earthly family. Imagine the awe and excitement among those early disciples!

Their lives became a vibrant expression of their faith. They shared meals, devoted themselves to learning, prayed earnestly, and cared for one another's needs. These acts of love and unity filled God's heart with joy, and as they lived out the principles of Acts 2:42-46, God kept His promise in verse 47, adding to their number daily those who were being saved.

A LASTING PROMISE

This incredible promise remains as true today as it was then. When we pattern our lives after the early church, even in something as simple as a Bible Talk in a living room, we can witness the same transformative results.

You don't need a massive crowd. A small group of faithful disciples, united in purpose and faith, creates a space for God to do extraordinary things.

In my city of Weston, Florida, I saw this truth come to life. Starting with just five people, our group grew to nearly fifty within a little under two years. The secret wasn't complicated: we lived out Acts 2:42-46 and trusted God to handle verse 47.

AN INVITATION

Right now, God is searching for individuals ready to help build His family in every corner of the world. This book is your guide to creating a thriving, purpose-driven community of believers wherever you are.

When a small group of committed disciples gathers with hearts set on God, miracles follow. The wonders recorded in the Bible can become realities in your own life.

As you take on the privilege of building this spiritual family, God's joy overflows. Your Bible Talk will become a beacon of hope and a critical part of expanding His kingdom.

Across centuries, from the early church to today, God has always sought willing hearts to carry out His mission. Now, He is calling you.

Will you step into this role? Will you help make God's eternal dream come true? The path is clear: build a community rooted in Acts 2:42-46, and watch God bring the growth described in verse 47.

Say yes to the journey. Step forward in faith, and prepare to be amazed by what God can do through your willingness to serve.

A TOUCH OF HEAVEN

You've likely picked up this book because you're considering leading a small group or have felt a nudge toward this calling. Before you read further, let me ask you a few questions:

- Would you like to build a close-knit group of Christian friends who love and support you, creating bonds that last a lifetime?
- How would it feel to help lead lost souls to salvation each month, introducing people to a relationship with God?
- Do you dream of being part of a movement where faith, joy, and spiritual growth flourish among people you love?
- Can you imagine leading a group filled with faith, fun, and fruitfulness, where you see lives transformed week after week?
- What if you could experience a taste of heaven every time your group met?

This is the heart of leading a Bible Talk. A small group of ordinary people, united by extraordinary faith, can become a powerhouse for glorifying God and saving souls. Great Bible Talk leaders inspire, guide, and create environments where God's kingdom grows, one Bible Talk at a time.

This book is about equipping anyone with the heart to serve to become the kind of leader who fosters a glimpse of heaven on Earth. It's a deeply rewarding yet challenging role. Not everyone will step up, but those who do will experience God's power in ways that change lives forever—yours included.

So, are you ready to be the leader God needs to build His kingdom, one Bible Talk at a time?

> *"Their leader will be one of their own; their ruler will arise from among them. I will bring him near and he will come close to me—for who is he who will devote himself to be close to me?" declares the Lord.*
>
> **—Jeremiah 30:21 NIV**

Chapter 1

What is a Bible Talk?

For where two or three gather in my name, there am I with them.

—Matthew 18:20 NIV

So, what exactly is a Bible Talk?

You might know it by other names like a small group, Soul Talk, Bible study, Christian Pow Wow, or catchy modern names like Soul Squad, Bliss Kingdom, Grace Gang, or Coffee with Jesus. Whatever the name, a Bible Talk is a small group of Christians with four main purposes:

1. Build faith in its members,
2. Create a loving family environment,
3. Enjoy meaningful fellowship and fun, and
4. Help more people come to know God.

Bible Talks provide something big church services often can't—a personal connection and close friendships. They also give you a purpose: working as a team to bring others to Christ.

HISTORY OF A MOVEMENT

In the early days of our movement, Bible Talks—also called "Soul Talks"—were the primary way to spread God's word. Campus and neighborhood Bible Talks became powerful tools, leading hundreds of people to become Christians.

Over time, these small groups started to do something even more incredible. Originally designed as a way to share the gospel, Bible Talks began transforming into tight-knit families of believers. People bonded deeply, formed lifelong friendships, and grew spiritually in ways that changed their lives.

Every week, members of these groups heard lessons that helped them build strong convictions. They made personal decisions to grow in faith, character, and action. These changes not only strengthened the group but also inspired them to share their faith, bringing new people into God's family.

These simple Bible Talks became the foundation of the church's growth. They weren't just adding numbers; they were creating communities rooted in love and mission. Over the years, these groups became the heart and soul of a thriving, joyful, and spiritually strong church.

THE FAMILY OF GOD AND THE ARMY OF GOD

A Bible Talk is a unique combination of two ideas: the Family of God and the Army of God. These two roles are like the wings of an airplane—both are needed to keep the group balanced and effective.

The Family of God focuses on love, connection, and support. It's about creating a safe space where people feel cared for, encouraged, and valued. On the other hand, the Army of God focuses on mission—going out to share the gospel and helping as many people as possible find salvation.

Sometimes, a group can lean too far to one side. If a Bible Talk becomes only about love and fellowship without reaching out to others, it's like firefighters who enjoy each other's company but don't respond to emergencies. There are so many people in the world who need saving, and a Bible Talk must have the courage and focus to reach them.

On the other hand, if a group is only focused on mission and neglects to care for its members, it can become cold and disconnected. God calls us to love one another, as Jesus said: **"By this everyone will know that you are my disciples, if you love one another."**—John 13:35 NIV

The key to a thriving Bible Talk is finding the balance. A great Bible Talk loves and supports its members while actively working to reach the lost. When both wings work together, God uses the group as a powerful force for His kingdom.

CONCLUSION

A Bible Talk is one of the most effective ways to build God's kingdom. It's a place where people can grow in faith, experience the love of a spiritual family, enjoy fun and meaningful connections, and help others find salvation.

Throughout history, Bible Talks have been the backbone of the church's growth. They provide something you can't find in a large gathering—a close-knit community where everyone feels valued and purposeful.

But leading a Bible Talk requires a special kind of heart. It takes passion, commitment, and faith to balance the Family of God and the Army of God. A great leader creates an environment where love and mission work hand in hand, inspiring everyone in the group to grow and serve.

In the next chapter, we'll dive deeper into what it takes to be the kind of leader who can guide a Bible Talk to fulfill its purpose. If you're ready to step into this role, let's explore how you can lead with a heart for God, people, and the mission He's called us to.

Chapter 2

The Heart of a
Bible Talk Leader

"I am the good shepherd. The good shepherd lays down his life for the sheep. The hired hand is not the shepherd and does not own the sheep. So when he sees the wolf coming, he abandons the sheep and runs away. Then the wolf attacks the flock and scatters it. The man runs away because he is a hired hand and cares nothing for the sheep. I am the good shepherd; I know my sheep and my sheep know me—just as the Father knows me and I know the Father—and I lay down my life for the sheep."

—John 10:11-15 NIV

Jesus called himself the good shepherd. By doing so, he set the standard for what it means to lead his people. He used himself as the ultimate example of a true spiritual leader in his church.

The good news is that Jesus made this standard clear and easy to understand. The challenging part is that living up to it is not easy. If you want to lead in Jesus' church, you must be willing to follow his example—and that means giving your all.

So, what did Jesus expect from his leaders? He only had one requirement: be willing to lay down your life for the sheep. No more, no less.

Jesus also explained what true leadership is not. He said the hired hand "did not own the sheep." In other words, if you want to lead Jesus' sheep, you must take ownership of them. Why? Because Jesus knew that people will only sacrifice for what they truly value.

To lead God's people today, you need a heart like Jesus'—a heart committed to being a good shepherd, and laying down your life for his sheep.

Let's begin by talking about the heart a Bible Talk leader needs.

A PASSION FOR GOD

"When it was almost time for the Jewish Passover, Jesus went up to Jerusalem. In the temple courts he found people selling cattle, sheep and doves, and others sitting at tables exchanging money. So he made a whip out of cords, and drove all from the temple courts, both sheep and cattle; he scattered the coins of the money changers and overturned their tables. To those who sold doves he said, 'Get these out

of here! Stop turning my Father's house into a market!' His disciples remembered that it is written: 'Zeal for your house will consume me.'"

—John 2:13-17 NIV

The first thing you need to lead God's people is a passion for God. This means having a zeal and energy that comes from an incredible love for Him.

Being a man or woman after God's own heart is essential because your goal is to lead people into a passionate and devoted relationship with their Creator. If you live with a deep love for God, your life will naturally inspire others to do the same.

A passion for God also fuels your commitment to righteousness. Like Jesus, you'll want to honor God in every area of your life. This means being open about your struggles and sins and fighting against anything that could harm your relationship with Him.

It also means standing up for what is right. Like Jesus in the temple, you'll have the courage to address sin when you see it. With love and truth, you'll challenge, encourage, and guide others to follow God's Word completely. This includes correcting and rebuking when necessary to help others live a life that pleases God.

A PASSION FOR PEOPLE

"When Jesus landed and saw a large crowd, he had compassion on them and healed their sick."

—Matthew 14:14 NIV

To lead people, you must have a passion for them. Why? Because your main job is taking care of people.

If you don't enjoy being around people, leading a Bible Talk will be very difficult. Trust me—I know this from experience. I'm an introvert by nature. For a long time, I was perfectly content with just me and God. But then the Bible showed me I couldn't call myself a disciple of Jesus without loving and caring for others.

Jesus said, **"If you love me, feed my sheep."** That meant I needed to grow in my love for people. So, I prayed for God to change my heart, and He did. Over time, I went from leading a small group of four people to leading a group of 120. If you pray to love people more, God will open your heart—and when He does, He'll give you more people to love.

A passion for people means going the extra mile to care for them, support them, and help them grow. It's about seeing their needs and doing whatever it takes to meet them. When you love people deeply, they feel it, and it makes all the difference in their spiritual journey.

A PASSION FOR SAVING THE LOST

> *"Jesus went through all the towns and villages, teaching in their synagogues, proclaiming the good news of the kingdom and healing every disease and sickness. When he saw the crowds, he had compassion on them, because they were harassed and helpless, like sheep without a shepherd. Then he said to his disciples, 'The harvest is plentiful but the workers are few. Ask the Lord of the harvest, therefore, to send out workers into his harvest field.'"*
>
> **—Matthew 9:35-38**

The third essential quality is a passion for saving the lost. Like Jesus, you need to have compassion for those who are far from God.

When you truly care about people, you can't stand by and do nothing while they're lost and hurting. Compassion moves you to action. It drives you to share the good news, help people understand God's love, and guide them toward salvation.

Compassion is what makes you willing to sacrifice your time, energy, and comfort to help others. It's what keeps you going, even when it's hard, because you desire nothing more than to help others and bring God joy by reuniting Him with His lost children.

Having a passion for the lost means you're always looking for opportunities to share your faith and help others come to know God. It's a labor of love that brings glory to God and transforms lives.

CONCLUSION

To be a great Bible Talk leader, you need to focus on your heart. Leadership is 90% about who you are and 10% about what you do.

If you want to lead well, strive to grow in your passion for God, your passion for people, and your passion for saving the lost. Even if you don't feel like you have these qualities now, don't worry. God will help you grow. As long as you're willing to try, He will make up the difference.

The people you lead will love you, not because you're perfect, but because of your heart to serve. So, let's work on developing the kind of heart that reflects Jesus—a heart full of love, passion, and commitment to building God's kingdom.

Chapter 3

The Roles of a
Bible Talk Leader

The word of the Lord came to me, saying, "Before I formed you in the womb I knew you, before you were born I set you apart; I appointed you as a prophet to the nations." "Alas, Sovereign Lord," I said, "I do not know how to speak; I am too young." But the Lord said to me, "Do not say, 'I am too young.' You must go to everyone I send you to and say whatever I command you. Do not be afraid of them, for I am with you and will rescue you," declares the Lord. Then the Lord reached out his hand and touched my mouth and said to me, "I have put my words in your mouth. See, today I appoint you over nations and kingdoms to uproot and tear down, to destroy and overthrow, to build and to plant."

—Jeremiah 1:4-9 NIV

If you're anything like me, you might feel hesitant about stepping into leadership. Maybe you've had thoughts like, "I'm not ready for this," or, "What if I'm not good enough?" Perhaps these excuses sound familiar:

- "I don't know if I can."
- "I think I'm too young."
- "I don't know enough yet."
- "I'm too sinful to lead anyone else."
- "Nobody's going to listen to me."
- "Please, find someone else."

If these thoughts resonate, you're in good company. Many great men of the Bible—Moses, Joshua, Gideon, Isaiah, Ezekiel, Jeremiah, and Peter—felt the same way. But God responded to them with reassurance, and He does the same for you:

> *"Have I not commanded you? Be strong and courageous. Do not be afraid; do not be discouraged, for the Lord your God will be with you wherever you go."*
>
> **—Joshua 1:9 NIV**

In other words, if you choose to lead in His Kingdom, God is saying:

> *"I have given you a role, and with that role comes responsibilities. If you dedicate yourself to fulfilling those responsibilities, I will always be with you. Follow Me, and you will succeed."*

The promise God gave to the prophets and leaders of old applies to you today. If you take on the role of a Bible Talk leader, God promises His presence and His help every step of the way:

> *"So do not fear, for I am with you; do not be dismayed, for I am your God. I will strengthen you and help you; I will uphold you with my righteous right hand."*
>
> **—Isaiah 41:10 NIV**

WITH GREAT POWER COMES GREAT RESPONSIBILITY

Now let's talk about what your roles and responsibilities will be as a Bible Talk leader.

A role is what is expected of you when you take on a responsibility. In other words, when you agree to lead a Bible Talk, you're accepting a set of expectations. In this chapter, I'll give you an overview of the six main roles of a Bible Talk leader. These will be explored in detail throughout the rest of this book, so by the end, you'll feel fully equipped to lead a great Bible Talk.

THE SIX ROLES OF A BIBLE TALK LEADER

1. Helping People Grow Close to God

Your first and greatest responsibility is helping the people in your Bible Talk grow closer to God. There is no higher purpose than helping someone love God with all their heart. If people are close to God, most of their spiritual and personal needs will naturally be met. This makes it easier to teach, train, and guide them to become more like Jesus.

2. Making Disciples of All Nations

Your second role is to help non-Christians commit to making Jesus Lord of their lives. Your Bible Talk is an extension of Jesus' mission to make disciples of all nations. The better you fulfill this role, the more you bring joy to God's heart.

3. Helping People Become More Like Jesus Through Effective Discipling

Discipling means teaching, correcting, training, and inspiring others to grow in their relationship with God. As a Bible Talk leader, you're responsible for helping each member become more like Jesus.

4. Building a Culture of Faith, Family, Fun, and Fruit

Your fourth responsibility is to create a culture where people feel like family. This means fostering an environment of faith, joy, love, and productivity. Your Bible Talk should be a safe place where people can grow spiritually, enjoy meaningful relationships, and experience God's love.

5. Delivering Engaging, Fun, and Convicting Bible Discussions

Leading Bible discussions that are engaging, fun, and convicting is your fifth role. These discussions are opportunities to build faith, inspire growth, and encourage non-Christians to explore a relationship with God.

6. Training New Bible Talk Leaders

Finally, you're responsible for training new leaders. As your Bible Talk grows, you'll need to multiply by raising up others who can lead their own groups. A great leader prepares others to take on the same responsibilities with faith and excellence.

CONCLUSION

To be an effective Bible Talk leader, you must excel in these six roles. They will help you create a group that loves God, loves one another, and brings glory to His name.

Now that you know the roles, let's dive deeper into the first and most important one: helping people grow close to God.

Chapter 4

Role #1—Helping People Grow Close to God

"When Enoch had lived 65 years, he became the father of Methuselah. After he became the father of Methuselah, Enoch walked faithfully with God for 300 years and had other sons and daughters. Altogether, Enoch lived a total of 365 years. Enoch walked faithfully with God; then he was no more, because God took him away."

—Genesis 5:21-24 NIV

"And the scripture was fulfilled that says, 'Abraham belie-ved God, and it was credited to him as righteousness,' and he was called God's friend."

—James 2:23 NIV

"The Lord would speak to Moses face to face, as one speaks to a friend."

—Exodus 33:11a NIV

*"After removing Saul, he made David their king. God testi-
fied concerning him: 'I have found David son of Jesse, a
man after my own heart; he will do everything I want him
to do.'"*

—Acts 13:22 NIV

*"The one who sent me is with me; he has not left me alone,
for I always do what pleases him."*

—John 8:29 NIV

W hat do all these verses have in common? They describe
men like Enoch, Abraham, Moses, David, and Jesus as having
a special closeness with God. Each of them had a relationship
so strong that God Himself called them His friends. Even Jesus,
to the shock of the Pharisees, referred to God as His Father—
something no one had dared to do before.

From the very beginning, God's desire has been to have
a close relationship with His children. Through Jesus, the
curtain in the temple has been torn, and now we have the
opportunity to approach God with confidence and build a
deep, personal connection with Him (Hebrews 4:16; 10:19-22).
God is eagerly waiting to draw near to us and connect with
us at the deepest level.

HELPING YOUR BIBLE TALK GROW CLOSE TO GOD

Helping the people in your Bible Talk grow closer to God is the most important role of a Bible Talk leader. When you help others strengthen their connection with God, you are fulfilling His greatest desire—to be close to His children now and for eternity (1 Timothy 2:3-4).

When your group members are close to God, it makes every other aspect of leadership easier and more enjoyable. Motivated by their love for God, they become eager to obey Him, making it simpler to guide them in living out their faith.

The opposite is also true. If someone's relationship with God is weak, leading them becomes far more challenging because they lack the motivation and strength to follow His commands. That's why this chapter is so crucial. Your ability to help your group grow closer to God will determine the overall success of your Bible Talk.

The good news is that most disciples genuinely want to grow closer to God. However, life's distractions can make it hard for them to stay focused. Your role as a Bible Talk leader is to help them prioritize their relationship with God and create space for it to grow.

As someone once said, **"The most important thing is to make sure the most important thing stays the most important thing."** Let's explore how you can help your group keep God as their top priority.

THE THREE KEYS TO HELPING YOUR BIBLE TALK GET CLOSER TO GOD

"Jesus replied: 'Love the Lord your God with all your heart and with all your soul and with all your mind. This is the first and greatest commandment.'"

—Matthew 22:37-38 NIV

There are three key ways to help your Bible Talk grow closer to God:

1. Ensuring everyone has daily quiet times and prayer.
2. Teaching them to connect emotionally with God.
3. Encouraging them to obey and put into practice what they learn.

1. Daily Quiet Times and Prayer

Quiet Time

Daily time spent in God's Word is essential for staying close to Him. Faith (Romans 10:17) and love for God (1 John 5:3) come from reading and obeying His Word. The Bible is the spiritual food that keeps our souls healthy and strong.

Just as our physical bodies need daily nourishment, our spiritual lives need consistent feeding through God's Word. Without it, we grow spiritually weak. Encouraging your group to prioritize quiet times helps them maintain their spiritual health.

Prayer

If the Bible is how God speaks to us, prayer is how we speak to Him. Together, they create a rich, ongoing conversation that deepens our relationship with Him. Like a loving father, God draws near when we pray (Deuteronomy 4:7).

Jesus Himself spent significant time in prayer (Mark 1:35; Luke 5:16; Luke 6:12). Some believe He prayed for hours each day. Through prayer, we pour out our hearts to God, praise Him, confess our sins, thank Him, and seek His help. This connects our hearts to His.

A helpful way to structure prayer is using the acronym **ACTS**:

1. **Adoration**: Praising and adoring God.
2. **Confession**: Admitting sins and seeking forgiveness.
3. **Thanksgiving**: Thanking God for His blessings.
4. **Supplication**: Bringing our needs and concerns to Him.

As a leader, inspire accountability by encouraging your group to prioritize quiet times and prayer. Daily check-ins, shared quiet times, and open discussions about the Bible can motivate and guide them.

2. Teaching How to Emotional Connect with God

While reading the Bible and praying are vital, they can become routine without an emotional connection to God. Teaching your group to pour out their hearts to Him—like David did—helps them form a deeper bond.

David's Psalms are filled with examples of his emotional vulnerability:

> *"You, God, are my God, earnestly I seek you; I thirst for you, my whole being longs for you, in a dry and parched land where there is no water."*
>
> **—Psalm 63:1 NIV**

David's ability to express his thoughts, struggles, and joys to God connected him deeply to the Lord. Encourage your group to do the same. One way is by praying with them, modeling vulnerability, and showing how to share their hearts with God.

3. Obeying and Applying God's Word

Hearing God's Word isn't enough; we must also put it into practice (James 1:22). Encourage your group to take what they learn and live it out in their daily lives. This not only strengthens their relationship with God but also deepens their faith and convictions.

CONCLUSION

Helping your Bible Talk grow closer to God is your most important responsibility. When you focus on this, every other role becomes easier. By encouraging daily quiet times and prayer, teaching emotional connection with God, and inspiring obedience to His Word, you create an environment where faith can thrive.

Lead by example, providing inspiring accountability and modeling a passionate relationship with God. Just as Jesus shaped His disciples, you can guide your group to become more like Him—deepening their connection with God and molding them into the image of Christ.

Chapter 5

Role #2—Making Disciples of All Nations (Part I)

Sharing Your Faith

"Then Jesus came to them and said, 'All authority in heaven and on earth has been given to me. Therefore go and make disciples of all nations, baptizing them in the name of the Father and of the Son and of the Holy Spirit, and teaching them to obey everything I have commanded you. And surely I am with you always, to the very end of the age.'"

—Matthew 28:18-20 NIV

The Great Commission in Matthew 28 makes it clear: the number one mission of a disciple of Jesus is to seek and save the lost. As a Bible Talk leader, your role is to inspire yourself and your group to fulfill this mission. This means rallying your team to go out, seek, and save the lost people in this world.

THE HEART TO SAVE THE WORLD

"Though I am free and belong to no one, I have made myself a slave to everyone, to win as many as possible. To the Jews I became like a Jew, to win the Jews. To those under the law I became like one under the law (though I myself am not under the law), so as to win those under the law. To those not having the law I became like one not having the law (though I am not free from God's law but am under Christ's law), so as to win those not having the law. To the weak I became weak, to win the weak. I have become all things to all people so that by all possible means I might save some. I do all this for the sake of the gospel, that I may share in its blessings."
—1 Corinthians 9:19-23 NIV

Imagine Paul living a quiet life in Tarsus, speaking occasionally at his local synagogue, and enjoying the comforts of home. Then, his friend Barnabas invites him to help a church full of Gentile Christians in Antioch. Paul could have chosen the easy path, but instead, he gave up his comforts and became a servant to everyone so he could save as many as possible.

Paul understood that on Judgment Day, careers, comforts, and quiet lives wouldn't matter—only the lives he helped save would. As Bible Talk leaders, we share this same mission. Our groups are an extension of the Great Commission, and our goal is to make disciples of all nations in our generation.

Making disciples of all nations can be broken down into three simple steps:

1. Sharing your faith and getting phone numbers.
2. Following up and inviting people to study the Bible.
3. Studying the Bible with them to help them make Jesus Lord of their lives.

This chapter focuses on the first step: sharing your faith.

SHARING YOUR FAITH

What does it mean to share your faith?

Sharing your faith means going out into the world, meeting people, and talking to them about God. It's that simple—though it's not always easy. But it doesn't have to feel awkward or difficult if you work smart and approach it with joy.

One of the best ways to inspire yourself and your group to share their faith is by energizing your group using the *Motivation Stack*:

1. Make it Meaningful.
2. Make it Easy.
3. Make it Fun.
4. Make it Rewarding and Satisfying

Make it Meaningful

When we know *why* we're doing something, it's easier to find the courage to do it. Remind your group of the big reasons sharing their faith matters:

- **Saving lives:** Sharing your faith can change someone's eternity.
- **Think about your own journey:** Help your group remember what their lives were like before they knew God.
- **God's family:** Show them that God longs to bring His children back to Him.
- **Gratitude:** Remind them how much God has done for them and how they can share that joy with others.

Make it Easy

When something feels hard, we're less likely to do it. Make sharing faith easier by removing barriers:

- **Start with people you know:** Friends, family, neighbors, or coworkers are great people to start with.
- **Go where people are:** Parks, coffee shops, or school campuses are full of opportunities to meet new people.
- **Make friends first:** Encourage your group to focus on building friendships. Talking about faith comes naturally once trust is built.
- **Use simple tools:** Invitations or flyers make it easier to share without feeling awkward.

- **Use social media:** Ask for prayers requests from their friends on social media. This usually makes it really easy to start a spiritual conversation.

Make it Fun

People love doing things that bring them joy. Add some fun to sharing faith to make it something your group looks forward to:

- **Go out together:** Sharing is easier with a buddy. Jesus sent His disciples out in pairs for a reason!
- **Mix sharing with hobbies:** Whether it's playing sports, crafting, or shopping, doing something you enjoy makes meeting people fun and natural.
- **Join groups or clubs:** Shared interests make starting conversations easier.
- **Turn it into a game:** Create fun challenges like a scavenger hunt or friendly competition to encourage your group.

Make it Rewarding and Satisfying

Everyone loves feeling like they've made a difference. Show your group the impact their efforts have:

- **Point to eternity:** Remind them that every effort to share faith makes God smile and stores up treasures in heaven.
- **Celebrate small wins:** Acknowledge when someone tries, even if it's just saying hello to a stranger.
- **Throw a party for big wins:** Celebrate baptisms and life changes so everyone feels part of the victory.

WHAT TO SAY

Sometimes the hardest part of sharing your faith is knowing what to say. Here's a simple process:

1. Be friendly and say hello.
2. Use an interesting opener, such as:
   - Are you a Christian?
   - Do you go to church?
   - Would you consider yourself a spiritually minded person?
   - What do you think God's plan is for your life?
3. Invite them to Bible Talk, church, or to study the Bible.
4. Gently challenge their objections.
5. Ask for their name and phone number.

Tip: One way I learned to help me get a lot of phone numbers is, while sharing my faith with someone, I'll pull out my phone and say, "Let me have your number," while looking at my phone and begin the process of taking their number down. This simple trick makes it easier for them to respond and give you their phone number.

PRACTICAL EVANGELISM GOALS

Daily Evangelism Goals

As a Bible Talk leader, aim to share your faith with 1-3 people a day. Consistency helps form a habit, making it easier to inspire others in your group to do the same.

Campus Evangelism Goals

For campus leaders, set a goal to share with 5-10 people daily, or even more at the start of the semester. College campuses are ideal for evangelism because they're full of people open to conversations.

Take your group with you when you share. They'll learn by watching your example, and even if they don't share as much at first, they'll eventually develop the habit.

CONCLUSION

Sharing our faith is one of the most important ways we fulfill the Great Commission and grow God's kingdom. It can feel intimidating at first, but it doesn't have to be complicated. Be friendly, start a conversation, invite people to Bible Talk or to study the Bible, and get their phone number to follow up.

Make sharing your faith a daily habit and teach your group to do the same. Go out with them, have fun, and celebrate each step. The more consistent you are, the more it becomes a part of who you are—and the better example you set for others.

With God's help, we can make a huge difference, one conversation at a time. Let's boldly share our faith, seek the lost, and grow our Bible Talks into vibrant communities that glorify God.

Chapter 6

Role #2—Making Disciples of All Nations (Part II)

Follow Up and Setting Up Bible Studies

"The wife of a man from the company of the prophets cried out to Elisha, 'Your servant my husband is dead, and you know that he revered the Lord. But now his creditor is coming to take my two boys as his slaves.' Elisha replied to her, 'How can I help you? Tell me, what do you have in your house?' 'Your servant has nothing there at all,' she said, 'except a small jar of olive oil.' Elisha said, 'Go around and ask all your neighbors for empty jars. Don't ask for just a few. Then go inside and shut the door behind you and your sons. Pour oil into all the jars, and as each is filled, put it to one side.' She left him and shut the door behind her and her sons. They brought the jars to her and she kept pouring. When all the jars were full, she said to her son, 'Bring me another one.' But he replied, 'There is not a jar left.' Then the oil stopped flowing."

—2 Kings 4:1-6 NIV

This inspiring story of the widow and the jars of oil teaches us a powerful lesson. The widow trusted God and was able to fill jar after jar with oil until she had no jars left. The flow of oil stopped only when there were no more jars to fill.

This story serves as a metaphor for how God works when we are making disciples. Like the oil that kept flowing, God will keep bringing conversions and baptisms as long as we have people actively studying the Bible. The moment we stop finding and setting up studies, the baptisms stop.

As Bible Talk leaders, it's our responsibility to keep the spiritual jars coming by consistently following up with people and setting up Bible studies. The more studies we have, the more opportunities God has to work through us to save lives and grow His Kingdom.

FOLLOWING UP WITH PEOPLE AND ASKING THEM TO STUDY THE BIBLE

Following up means reaching out to people who've shared their contact information and building a connection with them. It's about taking the relationship to the next level—inviting them to Bible Talk, church, coffee, or a Bible study.

The key to successful follow-up is showing a genuine interest in people. They gave you their number because they were open to connecting, so invest the time to learn about them and build trust. When people feel valued, they are more likely to be receptive to spiritual conversations.

Here's a simple system for effective follow-up:

HOW TO FOLLOW UP

1. **Set aside time:** Dedicate 15-30 minutes daily for follow-up calls.
2. **Use high energy:** Start the call with enthusiasm and positivity.
3. **Be personal:** Smile, use their name, and remind them where you met.
4. **Ask questions:** Show genuine interest by asking about their day, family, or interests. Share about yourself too.
5. **Reiterate your invitation:** Remind them of the invitation you gave them and ask if they'd like to come to Bible Talk.
6. **Highlight the benefits:** Explain why you love Bible Talk and why it could be meaningful for them.
7. **Confirm the plan:** If they agree to come, express your excitement and promise to follow up with a reminder.
8. **Send a confirmation:** Send a text or call the day before to confirm their attendance.

PRACTICAL FOLLOW-UP GOALS

The goal of follow-up is to secure a commitment. Whether it's attending Bible Talk, church, or a Bible study, a commitment is a verbal promise to take the next step. To inspire commitment, make your invitation engaging and personal. Share why you love Bible Talk and how it's helped you grow closer to God.

For example, you might say, *"How do you feel about your relationship with God? Would you be interested in taking it to the next level?"* If they say yes, follow up by asking, *"Great! Would you like to study the Bible?"*

HOW OFTEN SHOULD YOU FOLLOW UP?

Consistency is key. Set aside 3-4 times per week for follow-up calls. The best days are the days right before Bible Talk or Sunday service (e.g., Friday and Saturday). While daily follow-up is ideal, 3-4 sessions per week can still make a big impact.

ASKING PEOPLE TO STUDY THE BIBLE

The ultimate goal of follow-up is to help people study the Bible. The simplest way to do this is to **just ask.** Don't overthink it. Most people will either say yes or no, but the act of asking is what matters most.

It's often easier to ask after they've attended a Bible Talk or church service, but some people may be ready to study the Bible right away. Be bold and direct: *"Would you like to study the Bible and grow in your relationship with God?"*

Once they agree, set up a time, date, and place for the study.

SETTING UP A BIBLE STUDY

When scheduling a Bible study, simplify the process by offering two options: *"Are you free Wednesday or Thursday at 7:30 PM?"* This makes it easier for them to choose a time. If they aren't available, ask when they are free and adjust accordingly.

Prime Time: Most people are free during the evening (7:30-9:30 PM) or lunchtime for campus students (12-2 PM). Keep these times open to make scheduling bible studies easier.

Location: Choose a quiet, public place like a coffee shop or a non-crowded restaurant. Public settings also provide opportunities to share your faith with others. Alternatively, you can host studies at home, though you may miss the chance to inspire others around you.

Goals for Bible Studies

On average, it takes studying the Bible with about 10 people to find one person who will fully commit to Christ and be baptized. Therefore as the Bible Talk leader, a good goal is to set up a minimum of 2-3 new Bible studies each week. Consistently setting up new studies ensures that you'll always have opportunities to help save as many people as possible.

Here are some suggested weekly goals for your group based on life stages (for both men and women combined):

- **Singles:** 4-6 Bible studies per week
- **Married (no kids):** 2-4 Bible studies per week
- **Married (with kids):** 1-2 Bible studies per week

For campus Bible Talks, as the leader, aim for setting up 5-10 bible studies each week (that's about 20-40 studies per week as a group). On campuses, the flexibility of schedules, and the easy access to an abundance of people, allows for easily setting more studies, leading to more conversions each month.

CONCLUSION

Following up and setting up Bible studies are crucial for making disciples and growing your Bible Talk. Just like the widow's jars, as long as we keep setting up studies, the flow of conversions will continue.

Build genuine friendships, take a real interest in people's lives, and share why studying the Bible is meaningful to you. With boldness, love, and consistency, we can keep the spiritual oil flowing and help more people come to know Christ.

Let's go out and faithfully follow up, trusting God to add to our numbers daily as we make disciples, one Bible study at a time.

Chapter 7

Role #2—Making Disciples of All Nations (Part III)

Studying the Bible with People

"For we know, brothers and sisters loved by God, that he has chosen you, because our gospel came to you not simply with words but also with power, with the Holy Spirit and deep conviction. You know how we lived among you for your sake. You became imitators of us and of the Lord, for you welcomed the message in the midst of severe suffering with the joy given by the Holy Spirit. And so you became a model to all the believers in Macedonia and Achaia. The Lord's message rang out from you not only in Macedonia and Achaia—your faith in God has become known everywhere."

—1 Thessalonians 1:4-8 NIV

STUDYING THE BIBLE WITH PEOPLE

When it's time to sit down and study the Bible with someone, the ultimate goal is to help them make Jesus the Lord of their life. This may seem like a huge task, but like the saying goes, **"If you want to eat an elephant, take one small bite at a time."** Helping someone build faith and commit to Christ happens step by step.

Just like you wouldn't marry someone you just met, most people aren't ready to commit to Jesus right away. They need time to get to know God, understand His Word, and build their faith and love for Him. The process is much like a growing relationship—taking small, meaningful steps until they are ready to "tie the knot" through baptism and fully surrender their lives to God.

The best way to guide someone through this process is by using the **First Principles Bible Studies.** These studies are designed to help people understand what God expects from their lives, lead them to decisions of faith, and challenge them to take the next step.

For a copy of the First Principles Bible Studies click here: https://www.amazon.com/First-Principles-Follow-Studies-Small/dp/B08HGPPKFW

LEARNING THE FIRST PRINCIPLES STUDIES

As a Bible Talk leader, one of your key responsibilities is to learn how to effectively teach each study in the First Principles studies. From "Seeking God" to "Counting the Cost," you need to master each study so you can teach others effectively and train your Bible Talk members to do the same.

Ways to Learn the Studies

1. **Teach by doing:** The best way to learn is by studying the Bible with as many people as possible. Each study will deepen your understanding and help you refine your ability to guide others.
2. **Use quiet times:** If you don't have many studies set up, use your daily quiet time to review and memorize the studies. This will solidify your convictions and prepare you to teach.
3. **Memorize key points:** Commit to memory the scriptures, main points, and questions for each study. For example, during your commute, practice reciting the studies until you know them by heart.

By immersing yourself in these studies, you'll become confident in teaching them and better equipped to help others develop deep convictions.

MOVING HEARTS WITH THE 5 P'S

Helping someone make Jesus Lord requires not only teaching the Bible, but also moving their heart. While only God can truly change hearts, you can create the best environment for spiritual growth by focusing on the **5 P's**:

1. Prayer

> *"Opponents must be gently instructed, in the hope that God will grant them repentance leading them to a knowledge of the truth, and that they will come to their senses and escape from the trap of the devil, who has taken them captive to do his will."*
>
> **—2 Timothy 2:25-26 NIV**

The first and most powerful thing you can do is pray. Only God can grant repentance and open someone's heart to His truth. Pray for the person daily—before and after every study. Ask others in your Bible Talk to pray for them as well. Prayer moves God's heart, and He will work to move their heart, and help them overcome any obstacle standing in the way of their faith.

2. Preach the Word

> *"Is not my word like fire," declares the Lord, "and like a hammer that breaks a rock in pieces?"*
>
> **—Jeremiah 23:29 NIV**

God's Word is the key to transformation. While advice and persuasion have their place, true conviction comes from Scripture. Have a list of Bible passages ready to address common questions or doubts. Resources like OpenBible.info can help you find scriptures by topic. Let God's Word speak directly to their hearts.

3. Passion

"For we know, brothers and sisters loved by God, that he has chosen you, because our gospel came to you not simply with words but also with power, with the Holy Spirit and deep conviction."

—1 Thessalonians 1:4-5 NIV

Conviction isn't just taught—it's caught. Your passion and conviction are contagious. If you live as a sold-out disciple, your life will inspire others to do the same. When studying the bible, share your personal love for God and your commitment to Him with enthusiasm. In other words, don't just teach the scriptures, teach your convictions about the scriptions. This will encourage those you study with to develop their own convictions.

4. People

"God is love. Whoever lives in love lives in God, and God in them."
—1 John 4:16 NIV

Building a strong relationship with the person you're studying with is essential. People experience God's love through the love we show them. Spend time outside of studies building friendship and trust. Show genuine care for their lives, interests, and struggles. The more they feel God's love through you, the more their hearts will open to Him.

5. Persuasion

> *"With many other words he [Peter] warned them; and he pleaded with them, 'Save yourselves from this corrupt generation.'"*
>
> **—Acts 2:40 NIV**

The devil has spent years persuading people to believe lies. It's our job to lovingly help them see God's truth. Use scriptures, stories, and questions to challenge their thinking and dismantle false beliefs. Ask them to consider different perspectives, such as what God might think or how Satan might deceive them. Effective persuasion clears the way for faith to grow.

MONTHLY BIBLE STUDY GOALS

Setting clear goals about how many bible studies you will have monthly helps create momentum in your Bible Talk. Here are some targets to aim for:

- **Singles ministries:** Aim for helping 1-2 people become true, baptized disciples each month.
- **Campus ministries:** Aim for 2-4 baptisms monthly. With the flexibility of campus schedules, your potential is only limited by your effort and manpower.
- **Married ministries**: Aim for helping 1-2 people become true, baptized disciples every other month.

The key is to keep studying with as many people as possible and trust God to bring the growth.

CONCLUSION

Helping people make Jesus Lord is one of the greatest responsibilities of a Bible Talk leader. To do this effectively, you need to:

1. Master the **First Principles Bible Studies** so you can guide others through them with confidence.
2. Apply the **5 P's**: Pray for them, preach the Word, share your passion, build loving relationships, and lovingly persuade them toward truth.

When you faithfully invest in people's lives, God will work powerfully to transform hearts. Through prayer, scripture, passion, love, and persuasion, you'll see lives changed, one Bible study at a time. Let's trust God to add to His Kingdom as we continue to study His Word with boldness and love.

Chapter 8

Role #3—Helping People Grow Through Discipling

"He is the one we proclaim, admonishing and teaching everyone with all wisdom, so that we may present everyone fully mature in Christ."

— Colossians 1:28 NIV

THE ROLE OF DISCIPLING

One of your most significant roles as a Bible Talk leader is to disciple the men and women in your group. But what does discipling mean?

Discipling is when one person helps another grow in their relationship with God and become more like Jesus. It's about devoting yourself to training, guiding, and supporting someone. But it's also about building a deep, fulfilling friendship that strengthens over time.

The ability to influence and help others grow spiritually is a skill that develops with practice. This chapter will equip you with essential principles and practical guidelines to make discipling both impactful and rewarding.

DISCIPLING PRINCIPLES

Just as plants require sunlight, water, and good soil to thrive, people need the right environment to grow spiritually. These discipling principles are universal, working across cultures, ages, and life stages. Rooted in Scripture, they provide a framework for helping others grow into their full godly potential.

Discipling Principles in a Nutshell

1. Pray for them daily.
2. Pray for God to lead you.
3. Point them to God by using Scripture.
4. Speak the truth in love.
5. Build trust through empathy and understanding.
6. Share vulnerably from your life.
7. Meet consistently and often.
8. Lead by example and take them with you.
9. Be a friend.

1. Pray for Them Daily

The most powerful thing you can do for the person you disciple is to pray for them every day. Transformation comes from God, not us. Prayer invites His power to work in their life, softening their heart and guiding their steps.

Daily prayer also prepares their heart for your conversations, making your role much easier as God has already been at work.

2. Pray for God to Lead You

Every person you disciple will face unique challenges. Knowing what to say and how to help them can feel overwhelming. That's why prayer is essential. Ask God for wisdom, love, and guidance before each meeting.

When you rely on God, He will provide insights and words that deeply impact the person you're discipling. Remember, you have the Creator of the universe backing you up!

3. Point Them to God Using Scripture

Your role is to help others grow closer to God, and point them to God, not to yourself. While personal advice has its place, it's God's Word that brings true transformation. Share scriptures abundantly in your conversations. The Bible builds faith, reveals God's character, and teaches people to rely on Him.

If you're worried about not knowing the right scriptures, tools like OpenBible.info can help you find relevant verses for almost any topic. Remember, our goal is to guide people toward Jesus, not to ourselves.

4. Speak the Truth in Love

Discipling sometimes requires hard conversations. But love means speaking the truth, even when it's uncomfortable. People need to know where they are spiritually to grow closer to God.

Imagine this: If a friend saw a deadly scorpion crawl into your shoe but said nothing to avoid conflict, how would you feel after being stung? Similarly, sin is like the scorpion, and avoiding hard truths can lead to spiritual harm. Speak up, but always with love and gentleness.

5. Build Trust Through Empathy

Without trust, there can be no influence. People need to know you genuinely care before they'll listen to you. Empathy—the effort to understand and value someone's feelings—builds this trust.

Show empathy by:

- Actively listening and reflecting back what they share.
- Giving your undivided attention.
- Reassuring them they are not alone.
- Letting them know you pray for them specifically.

When people feel understood and valued, they become more open to growth and change.

6. Share Vulnerably from Your Life

Vulnerability fosters connection. When you share your struggles, mistakes, and how God has helped you, it creates a safe space for others to open up about their challenges too.

Be mindful of what the person can handle, but don't shy away from showing your humanity. Vulnerability breaks down walls and helps people see that they're not alone in their struggles.

7. Meet Consistently and Speak Often

Consistency is key to spiritual growth. Weekly discipling times (about an hour) paired with brief daily encouragement (10-15 minutes) can have a profound impact.

Regular meetings create a rhythm of accountability, support, and growth. Daily check-ins can be as simple as a quick call or text to share encouragement or ask how they're doing spiritually.

8. Lead by Example and Take Them with You

Jesus trained His disciples by letting them walk alongside Him. You can do the same. Invite the person you disciple to join you in your daily life. Whether it's sharing your faith, praying, or simply spending time together, your example will teach them more than words ever could.

Don't just show your strengths; let them see how you handle struggles, too. This transparency will inspire them to persevere in their own challenges.

9. Be a Friend

Discipling isn't just about spiritual training—it's about building deep, lasting friendships. As you walk alongside someone in their spiritual journey, you'll form bonds that can last a lifetime.

Proactively pursue friendship by sharing your life, celebrating victories, and supporting them through challenges. Love is the foundation of all discipleship, and friendship is one of its greatest expressions.

DISCIPLING FRAMEWORK: THE 5 QUESTIONS

Here's a simple framework of discussion questions to make your discipling times the most impactful experience for the person you are discipling:

1. How was your week?
2. How's your relationship with God going?
3. Do you have any sins or temptations to confess?
4. How's it going sharing your faith and getting Bible studies?
5. How's the rest of your life going?

These questions cover the most critical aspects of spiritual life and provide a well-rounded structure for your conversations.

CONCLUSION

Helping someone grow closer to God and become more like Jesus is one of the most rewarding experiences you'll ever have. By applying these principles and using this framework, you can create an environment where people thrive spiritually.

As Jesus commanded, **"Teach them to obey everything I have commanded you."** By investing in others, you'll not only help them grow but also experience the joy of fulfilling God's purpose for your life. Together, let's train, encourage, and inspire others to walk faithfully with God.

Chapter 9

Role #4—Building a Spiritual and Loving Culture (Part I)

"A new command I give you: Love one another. As I have loved you, so you must love one another. By this everyone will know that you are my disciples, if you love one another."

—John 13:34-35 NIV

Now we turn to what is perhaps the most joyful and rewarding role of leading a Bible Talk: building a culture of the four Fs—faith, family, fun, and fruit. This is where the beauty of small groups truly shines.

When a visitor steps into a Bible Talk and experiences the love among the members, hears the Word being preached, and feels the warmth and joy of fellowship, it leaves a profound impact on their heart. It helps them see and feel the love of God through the people they encounter, compelling them to want to belong to the group and ultimately to make Jesus Lord of their lives.

The blueprint for this culture is beautifully laid out in Acts 2:42-47:

> *"They devoted themselves to the apostles' teaching and to fellowship, to the breaking of bread and to prayer. Everyone was filled with awe at the many wonders and signs performed by the apostles. All the believers were together and had everything in common. They sold property and possessions to give to anyone who had need. Every day they continued to meet together in the temple courts. They broke bread in their homes and ate together with glad and sincere hearts, praising God and enjoying the favor of all the people. And the Lord added to their number daily those who were being saved."*

This passage shows us that when a group devotes itself to the principles of Acts 2:42-46, God responds by fulfilling verse 47. In the same way, if we follow this biblical pattern, our small groups can see God add to our number daily, those who are being saved. The key is building a group that thrives on faith, family, fun, and fruit.

FAITH

Faith is the foundation of any thriving small group, and the Bible tells us how to grow it in Romans 10:17:

> *"Consequently, faith comes from hearing the message, and the message is heard through the word about Christ."*

A steady diet of God's Word is essential to build faith in your group. Here are some ways to ensure scripture is consistently shared:

Weekly Bible Discussions

Regular group Bible discussions allow members and visitors to dive into the Word together. Hearing different perspectives deepens understanding and conviction. These discussions create an environment where faith is not just taught but also caught through shared insights and engagement.

Weekly Church Events

Consistent attendance at church services, midweeks, or devotionals strengthens faith as members receive biblical teaching and fellowship. Encourage your group to prioritize these events, offering gentle accountability to help them see the value these gatherings bring to their spiritual growth.

Weekly Discipling Times and Daily Encouragement

Personal discipling times and daily check-ins keep members spiritually fed and inspired. A simple call or text with a scripture can work wonders in helping faith grow, showing that God's Word is actively at work in their lives.

FAMILY AND FUN

Creating a family atmosphere where members feel loved, supported, and cared for is vital to a thriving Bible Talk. Jesus commanded this in John 13:34-35:

> *"Love one another. As I have loved you, so you must love one another."*

To foster this environment, plan intentional opportunities for members to connect, serve, and celebrate life together.

Monthly Family Times

Plan monthly events that allow the group to relax and bond. Whether it's a picnic, a game night, or a group outing, these times of fun and fellowship build trust and deepen relationships. Add food and music to make the time even more memorable.

Sharing Faith Together

Going out as a group to share your faith creates unique bonding experiences. It builds camaraderie, strengthens shared purpose, and gives members opportunities to encourage one another. Gamify the experience to make it even more enjoyable.

Doing Ministry Together

Collaborating on ministry activities, from organizing events to helping someone study the Bible, unites the group in their mission. These shared sacrifices and victories create lasting bonds and deepen spiritual friendships.

Celebrating Special Days

Marking birthdays, anniversaries, or achievements helps members feel valued and loved. Celebrating together strengthens the sense of family and creates joyful memories that last a lifetime.

Hang Out Together

Using every opportunity to spend time together will build bonds that will last a lifetime. Whether that's going to lunch after church, having breakfast before work, an impromptu road trip, or a Sunday night barbeque—these special moments create memories that will knit your hearts together on the deepest levels.

FRUIT

A group that thrives on faith, family, and fun will naturally be fruitful. When everyone works together, contributing their time, talents, and resources, it creates an environment where God can move powerfully to bring about conversions.

Encourage everyone to share their faith, join Bible studies, and pray for those studying the Bible. Unity and shared purpose amplify the group's impact, as Genesis 11:6 reminds us:

> *"If as one people speaking the same language they have begun to do this, then nothing they plan to do will be impossible for them."*

Provide opportunities for everyone to participate in the mission, whether it's through pairing up to share their faith, inviting them to Bible studies, or having them encourage those studying the Bible. The more engaged the group is, the more fruit they will bear.

CONCLUSION

Building a culture of faith, family, fun, and fruit is about following the example of the early church in Acts 2. When we devote ourselves to the apostles' teaching, fellowship, prayer, and breaking bread together, God blesses the effort by adding to our number daily. Let's work together to create groups that reflect the love, joy, and mission of Jesus, and watch as God transforms lives through the culture we build.

Chapter 10

Role #4—Building a Spiritual and Loving Culture (Part II)

"Love must be sincere. Hate what is evil; cling to what is good. Be devoted to one another in love. Honor one another above yourselves."

—Romans 12:9-10 NIV

To establish the best culture for God to work powerfully in your Bible Talk, you need to anchor it on two guiding spiritual principles. These principles serve as the foundation for creating an Acts 2:42-46 environment that compels God to act as described in verse 47. Without these principles, your Bible Talk will falter. With them, you create fertile ground for God to work miracles.

These foundational principles are:

1. Building a Righteous Culture
2. Building a Culture of Love and Empathy

In this chapter, we'll dive into both principles, exploring how to cultivate a culture of spiritual growth and genuine love.

BUILDING A RIGHTEOUS CULTURE

A spiritual and righteous culture leads people to greater devotion and obedience to God. To cultivate this, you need three critical elements:

1. **100% Obedience to God and His Word**
2. **Zero Tolerance for Sin**
3. **Everyone Involved in Doing God's Work**

100% Obedience to God and His Word

Throughout Scripture, God calls His people to wholehearted obedience. This must be the standard for your Bible Talk.

Reinforce this standard by preaching and teaching lessons that highlight God's expectation of wholeheartedness. Teach against lukewarm Christianity, half-heartedness, and the dangers of comparing ourselves to others instead of striving to be like Jesus. Use examples from Scripture to inspire growth and demonstrate that God's standard is achievable through love and dedication.

However, remember to balance the challenge with encouragement. Some disciples have sensitive consciences and may feel overwhelmed by their shortcomings. Remind them of God's mercy and inspire them to grow out of love for Him, not fear.

Zero Tolerance for Unrepentant Sin

Sin is like a harmful toxin—it spreads, weakens, and destroys. Just as you wouldn't tolerate a dangerous parasite in your body, you can't allow sin to linger in Jesus' spiritual body.

This doesn't mean condemning people but lovingly calling them to repentance. Use prayer and Scripture to help them see their sin, and point them back to the cross and their commitment to Jesus as Lord. Share your own struggles and victories to encourage them. Remember, the goal is not punishment but restoration.

By fostering a zero-tolerance attitude toward sin, you create an environment where righteousness thrives and God's presence abounds.

Everyone Involved in Doing God's Work

A healthy Bible Talk is not a one-person show. Everyone must play a role in God's mission.

Encourage participation by identifying people's talents and assigning them responsibilities that align with their skills. For example, someone with artistic talent can design group invitations, while someone with a gift for hospitality can host meetings.

Also, involve every member in weekly Bible studies. Not only does this deepen their faith, but it also strengthens their commitment to the group's mission. Take members with you to share your faith, serve others, or encourage brothers and sisters. The more they engage, the more they'll feel a sense of purpose and belonging.

BUILDING A CULTURE OF LOVE AND EMPATHY

Love and empathy are the lifeblood of a thriving spiritual community. Just as a fish cannot survive out of water, disciples cannot flourish without a loving and empathetic environment.

God Himself is love, and His family must reflect that love. A culture without empathy suffocates spiritual growth, but one rooted in love and understanding becomes a place where disciples thrive and lost souls are drawn.

What Is Empathy?

Empathy is the effort to understand and value another person's pain, making them feel supported and not alone. It's as simple as saying, "I've been there" or "I'm here for you." Empathy is not about solving every problem—it's about showing that you care.

The following are some habits that if you practice them, can build abundant empathy in your group.

Being Vulnerable
Vulnerability is powerful. When you share your struggles, weaknesses, and mistakes, you create a safe environment where others feel free to do the same. It dismantles shame and fosters deep connections.

By being the first to open up, you set the tone for the group. Your honesty invites others to take off their masks and seek the help they need to grow. To build courage for vulnerability, practice opening up to God in prayer. His unconditional love will empower you to share openly with others, knowing His acceptance is all that matters.

Showing Abundant Grace

Mistakes are inevitable. How you respond to them determines the culture of your group. Will it be a culture of fear or one of grace and growth?

Grace creates an environment where people feel safe enough to acknowledge their mistakes and seek help. Instead of rushing to correct them, listen, empathize, and assure them they're not alone. A simple "I've been there" can make all the difference. Share your own experiences to build rapport and trust. Once they feel safe, they'll be more open to the guidance they need.

Expressing Genuine Interest

In a self-centered world, showing genuine care for others stands out as a beacon of God's love. Small acts of kindness can have a profound impact:

- **Give your full attention.** When someone speaks, listen intently, making them feel valued.
- **Ask thoughtful questions.** Go beyond surface-level conversations to show that you care about their life and struggles.

- **Avoid judgment.** Instead, seek to understand their perspective and feelings. A simple "That sounds really hard" or "I can't imagine how tough that must be" communicates empathy and care.

CONCLUSION

Building a spiritual culture and a culture of empathy is about balancing righteousness with love. By calling your Bible Talk to 100% obedience to God and ensuring everyone is engaged in His work, you establish a foundation of spiritual growth. By fostering empathy through vulnerability, grace, and genuine interest, you create an environment where people feel safe, loved, and inspired to grow.

When your group reflects God's love and righteousness, it becomes a place where disciples flourish and lost souls are drawn. And just like in Acts 2, God will bless your efforts by adding to your number daily those who are being saved.

Chapter 11

Role #5—Delivering Fun, Engaging, and Deeply Convicting Bible Discussions

"Paul entered the synagogue and spoke boldly there for three months, arguing persuasively about the kingdom of God. But some of them became obstinate; they refused to believe and publicly maligned the Way. So Paul left them. He took the disciples with him and had discussions daily in the lecture hall of Tyrannus. This went on for two years, so that all the Jews and Greeks who lived in the province of Asia heard the word of the Lord."

—Acts 19:8-10 NIV

This passage shows us the incredible power of Bible discussions. Paul used a simple but effective approach: consistent, engaging conversations about Jesus in the lecture hall of Tyrannus. Over time, the Word of God spread throughout the province of Asia. This teaches us that small group Bible discussions, when done well, can have an enormous impact, transforming lives, communities, and even entire regions.

While there are many important aspects to leading a Bible Talk, delivering fun, engaging, and deeply convicting Bible discussions is one of the most crucial. These discussions not only inspire people to study the Bible but also keep them coming back week after week, hungry to learn and grow.

The best Bible discussions inspire and nurture people, increasing their desire to return and grow spiritually. To achieve this, your Bible discussions must **FEED** your group:

1. **F**—Fun
2. **E**—Entertaining
3. **E**—Engaging
4. **D**—Deeply Convicting

BIBLE DISCUSSIONS MUST BE FUN AND ENTERTAINING

"To take people on a journey, you first need to get them on the bus."

Before people are willing to listen and learn, you need to capture their attention and interest. Fun and entertainment are the most effective ways to do this because everyone enjoys a good time. When your discussions are fun, people are more open to participating and absorbing the message.

Here are some ways to add fun and entertaining elements to your Bible Talk:

- **Fun Ice Breaker Questions**: Start with lighthearted questions to get everyone laughing and relaxed.
- **Metaphors and Stories**: Use relatable and humorous anecdotes to connect with your audience.
- **Jokes**: Tasteful humor can lighten the mood and create a warm atmosphere.
- **Funny Lists from the Internet**: Share amusing lists that relate to your topic.
- **Games**: Incorporate simple group games to energize the room.
- **Props**: Visual aids or quirky objects can make lessons memorable.
- **Videos**: Show short, funny, or thought-provoking clips to set the tone.
- **Role-Playing**: Engage participants by acting out Bible stories or scenarios.

The key is to know your audience and tailor the fun to their interests. When people enjoy themselves, they'll be more open to the deeper spiritual truths you'll share.

BIBLE DISCUSSIONS MUST BE ENGAGING

A Bible Talk should feel like a dynamic conversation, not a lecture. The goal is to draw people in with thought-provoking questions that make them think deeply about God's Word and how it applies to their lives.

Here are some questions that work well for any Bible discussion:

1. What can we learn about God/Jesus from this passage?
2. What do you think God/Jesus is trying to teach us here?
3. What did you like about this passage?
4. What did you find challenging about this passage?
5. How can you obey this teaching in your life?
6. How will you apply this lesson this week?
7. What's your biggest takeaway from today's discussion?
8. Who will you share this lesson with?

When you tailor your questions to your group's specific stage of life (e.g., singles, married couples, college students), you'll see even greater engagement. Thought-provoking questions invite everyone to participate, making the discussion more impactful and memorable.

BIBLE DISCUSSIONS MUST BE DEEPLY CONVICTING

The most important aspect of a Bible Talk is its ability to convict hearts. Fun and engagement might draw people in, but conviction is what changes lives. Disciples are looking for experiences that challenge and transform them, helping them grow to be more like Jesus.

How to Make Your Discussions Convicting

1. Compare to Godly Examples

Present stories of godly men and women in the Bible, then challenge your group to measure their own lives against these examples. For example, Acts 5:40-42 says:

> "His speech persuaded them. They called the apostles in and had them flogged. Then they ordered them not to speak in the name of Jesus, and let them go. The apostles left the Sanhedrin, rejoicing because they had been counted worthy of suffering disgrace for the Name. Day after day, in the temple courts and from house to house, they never stopped teaching and proclaiming the good news that Jesus is the Messiah."

You can ask: *The apostles, even after being whipped, shared their faith daily. How many people have you shared your faith with this week? What excuses are holding you back, and how do you think the apostles would respond to your excuses?"*

2. Contrast with Ungodly Examples

Show similarities between your audience and ungodly characters in the Bible to highlight areas for growth. For example you can say:

"In Mark 10, the Rich Young Ruler walked away from Jesus because he wasn't willing to give up one thing. What's the one thing in your life that's holding you back from wholeheartedly following Jesus? Is it worth missing out on eternity for?"

3. Help Them See Through God's Eyes

Use metaphors to help your audience understand how God views their actions. For example you can say:

"According to 1 Timothy 2:3-4, God wants all men to be saved. Imagine you've lost your child. How would you feel if the police refused to help because they were too busy or uncomfortable? Now think about how God feels when we don't seek out His lost children because we're too busy or uncomfortable."

CALL THEM TO A DECISION

Every Bible discussion should end with a clear call to action. Challenge your group to repent of sin, change a habit, or follow Jesus more wholeheartedly. Be bold yet loving, encouraging them to take specific steps to grow in their faith.

Remember, the bible will be rendered powerless in people's lives if people don't put it to practice. But when they put it to practice, it is transformative. Therefore you have to make your Bible Talk a place where people go, not just to know or learn something—but a place where people go to DO something.

CONCLUSION

Delivering fun, engaging, and deeply convicting Bible discussions is one of the most powerful ways to grow your Bible Talk and change lives. By incorporating the **FEED** elements—fun, entertainment, engagement, and conviction—you'll create discussions that inspire people to come back week after week and apply God's Word to their lives.

Put in the effort to make your Bible Talks creative, memorable, and spiritually impactful. With God's help, your discussions will not only strengthen the faith of your group but also draw more souls into His kingdom. Let's commit to giving our best and trust God to work through every discussion to bring transformation and growth.

For a list of 12 powerful Bible Talk Discussion you can start with, go to the Appendix.

Chapter 12

Role #6—Raising Up Bible Talk Leaders

"And the things you have heard me say in the presence of many witnesses entrust to reliable people who will also be qualified to teach others."

—2 Timothy 2:2

One of the most important responsibilities of a Bible Talk Leader is raising up future leaders who can carry on the mission. Why? Because a successful Bible Talk will grow. As it grows larger, it can lose the intimacy and personal connection that makes small groups so effective. A larger group also becomes harder to manage, making it more challenging to provide individual attention to every member.

The solution? Splitting the Bible Talk into smaller, more intimate groups. For this to happen, you must identify, train, and equip reliable people who can lead these new groups with the same heart and vision. This principle is echoed in 2 Timothy 2:1-2, where Paul urges Timothy to entrust his teachings to others who are faithful and capable of teaching as well.

Let's explore how to identify potential leaders, train them, and prepare them to take on the incredible responsibility of leading a Bible Talk.

IDENTIFYING LEADERS: THE FAITH FRAMEWORK

When looking for future leaders, the most essential quality to seek is **FAITH**. A leader must demonstrate that they are:

1. **F**—Faithful
2. **A**—Available
3. **I**—Initiates
4. **T**—Teachable
5. **H**—Heart for God and People

Faithful

A potential leader must have a strong, consistent relationship with God. This includes daily Bible reading, prayer, openness about sin and temptation, and wholehearted obedience to God's Word. Since the leader sets the example for the entire group, this is non-negotiable.

Available

A leader must be willing to invest time and energy into the group. This includes having quiet times with members, sharing their faith, discipling others, and attending Bible Talk Leader training meetings. Faithful disciples often find joy, not burden, in sacrificing for God's people, making availability a natural extension of their commitment to God.

Initiates

Leadership requires proactivity. A good leader takes ownership of the group, making decisions and taking action without constant guidance. They must see the Bible Talk as their spiritual family and feel a personal responsibility for its growth and well-being.

Teachable

Humility is critical. A teachable leader is eager to learn, willing to be corrected, and open to growing in their understanding of God's Word and leadership principles. This balance of independence and interdependence creates a leader who is both creative and collaborative.

Heart for God and People

Ultimately, the most important quality is a deep love for God and others. A leader with a strong heart for God will prioritize pleasing Him above all else, while a heart for people will guide them to make decisions that benefit the group. Talent is valuable, but a leader with a heart for God and people is indispensable.

SELECTING THE LEADER

Many people don't naturally see themselves as leaders. That's why it's essential to approach them personally, share your vision for their potential, and encourage them to step into the role.

You can do this by having an "Elijah and Elisha" talk. Refer to 1 Kings 19:19-21, where Elijah called Elisha to follow him and become his apprentice. Use this story to inspire your chosen leader, emphasizing the qualities you see in them and explaining the responsibilities of a Bible Talk Leader.

Share your expectations:

1. Outline the roles and responsibilities of a Bible Talk Leader.
2. Describe the training process they will undergo.
3. Emphasize the need for humility and teachability.
4. Communicate your belief in their ability to succeed.

If they accept, you can officially begin their training journey.

MAKING IT OFFICIAL: BIBLE TALK ASSISTANT

To help the new leader ease into their role, start by appointing them as a **Bible Talk Assistant**. This gives them the chance to practice leadership in a smaller capacity while gaining confidence and experience.

Announce it to the group: Let everyone know that this individual will be serving as your assistant, with the goal of eventually leading their own Bible Talk. This builds credibility and prepares the group for a future transition.

Practical responsibilities for an assistant:

1. **Bible Discussions**: Lead the discussion once a month or biweekly.
2. **Bible Studies**: Take the lead in early First Principles studies and gradually handle more complex studies.
3. **Discipling**: Assign them one or two people to disciple.
4. **Mentoring**: Have them guide younger or weaker members in basic discipleship habits.
5. **Follow-Up**: Let them lead follow-up studies with new disciples.

This gradual approach ensures that they gain hands-on experience while still having your guidance and support.

TRAINING A BIBLE TALK LEADER

Effective training involves a combination of observation, practice, and reflection. Here are three key methods:

1. Take Them With You

> *"About eight days after Jesus said this, he took Peter, John and James with him and went up onto a mountain to pray."*
> **—Luke 9:28**

Just as Jesus trained His apostles by bringing them along, you should involve your trainee in every aspect of Bible Talk leadership. Let them observe you during:

- Quiet times and prayer
- Sharing faith
- Bible studies
- Discipling sessions
- Planning and leading discussions

By experiencing your leadership firsthand, they'll gain invaluable insights that can't be learned from a book or a lecture.

2. Debrief After Every Experience

> *"The apostles gathered around Jesus and reported to him all they had done and taught."*
> **—Mark 6:30**

After each leadership experience, take time to debrief. Ask questions like:

- What did you learn from this experience?
- Why do you think I made certain decisions?
- How does this align with biblical principles?
- How would you handle a similar situation in the future?

Debriefing helps solidify their learning and gives them the confidence to take on more responsibility.

3. See One, Do One, Teach One

This method, commonly used in the medical field, is highly effective for leadership training:

- **See One**: Have them watch you perform a task multiple times to understand how it's done.
- **Do One**: Allow them to practice the task with your support and guidance.
- **Teach One**: Once they've mastered the task, ask them to teach it to someone else.

This process accelerates learning, deepens understanding, and builds confidence.

CONCLUSION

Raising up Bible Talk Leaders is one of the most rewarding aspects of leadership. It not only allows your group to grow and multiply but also creates opportunities for others to use their gifts for God's glory.

By identifying leaders with FAITH, equipping them through hands-on training, and gradually increasing their responsibilities, you'll prepare them to lead with confidence and conviction. Together, you'll expand God's kingdom, one Bible Talk at a time, turning a mustard seed of faith into a thriving tree where others can find shelter and hope (Matthew 13:31-32).

Chapter 13

Training Your Bible Talk
to Work as a Team

"A few days later, when Jesus again entered Capernaum, the people heard that he had come home. They gathered in such large numbers that there was no room left, not even outside the door, and he preached the word to them. Some men came, bringing to him a paralyzed man, carried by four of them. Since they could not get him to Jesus because of the crowd, they made an opening in the roof above Jesus by digging through it and then lowered the mat the man was lying on. When Jesus saw their faith, he said to the paralyzed man, 'Son, your sins are forgiven.'"

—Mark 2:1-5

"The Lord said, 'If as one people speaking the same language they have begun to do this, then nothing they plan to do will be impossible for them.'"

—Genesis 11:6

The power of your Bible Talk comes from your group's ability to work as a team. No amount of individual talent or effort can match the collective impact of a united, purpose-driven team working together for God's mission.

Even Jesus, the Son of God, didn't work alone. He could have easily carried out His ministry by Himself, but instead, He built a team—a tight-knit group of men and women who would carry His mission forward after His ascension. That team changed the world.

As a Bible Talk Leader, you have the privilege and responsibility of transforming a group of unique individuals with different backgrounds, personalities, and perspectives into a cohesive team that can achieve extraordinary results for God's kingdom. It's challenging, but it's also one of the most rewarding aspects of leadership.

Here are some practical guidelines to help you turn your Bible Talk into a unified and effective team.

KEYS TO TRAINING YOUR BIBLE TALK TO BE A GREAT TEAM

Building a strong team requires intentional effort. While personality compatibility and character play a role, the spiritual unity of your group as disciples of Jesus provides a solid foundation. Everyone in the group shares a common purpose: to love God, love others, and fulfill the Great Commission.

To harness this unity and grow together as a team, focus on these three keys:

1. **Create opportunities for the group to grow together.**
2. **Assign everyone a role (The 4 Ps).**
3. **Commit to incremental improvement.**

1. Create Opportunities for the Group to Grow Together

Shared experiences build bonds. Whether your group is working on a task, planning an event, or enjoying fellowship, the time they spend together strengthens their relationships and fosters teamwork.

Meaningful projects create the strongest bonds. Serving together—whether it's sharing your faith, studying the Bible with someone, or helping the poor—gives your group a sense of shared purpose. These experiences create deep connections and lasting memories.

For example, pairing members to work together on projects like organizing refreshments, setting up for Bible Talk, or cleaning up after a meeting fosters collaboration and mutual support.

Have fun together. Fun activities can also bring people closer. Whether it's a game night, karaoke, or a casual hangout, these moments allow members to see each other's personalities, build trust, and develop deeper friendships. Plan regular fun events, and involve different members in the planning process to encourage teamwork.

2. Assign Everyone a Role (The 4 Ps)

Every successful team has clear roles. In your Bible Talk, you can identify roles based on the natural strengths and personalities of your members. I call these the **4 Ps**:

1. **Producer**: The person who sets the example, gets things done, and produces results.
2. **Planner**: The person who is skilled at organizing events, managing details, and keeping the group on track.
3. **People Person**: The person who excels at building relationships, making others feel welcome, and creating a sense of family.
4. **Partier**: The person who knows how to have fun and create enjoyable activities for the group.

Assigning roles not only helps the group function more effectively but also gives each member a sense of purpose and ownership. People are naturally more engaged and joyful when they feel they're contributing in a way that aligns with their strengths.

Take time to get to know your members' talents and personalities. Ask questions, observe their interactions, and help them discover where they can thrive. Once roles are assigned, encourage each person to embrace their responsibilities and work together toward the group's goals.

3. Commit to Incremental Improvement

Building a strong team doesn't happen overnight. It requires patience, persistence, and a commitment to consistent growth.

Adopt a mindset of **incremental improvement**—helping your team grow by 1% each week. While small progress may seem insignificant at first, it compounds over time and leads to extra-ordinary results.

Celebrate the small wins. Acknowledge and encourage even the smallest steps forward. When people feel their progress is recognized, they're more motivated to continue growing.

Provide "gentle pressure persistently applied." Growth often requires a mix of encouragement and challenge. Be patient as your members learn and develop, but consistently guide them toward higher levels of maturity and effectiveness.

Break goals into manageable steps. Help your members identify areas they want to grow in, and create a plan with clear, actionable steps. For example, if someone wants to grow in sharing their faith, start with simple challenges like inviting one person to Bible Talk each week.

Over time, you'll witness incredible transformation in your team. People who once doubted their abilities will step into leadership roles. Members who were initially hesitant to serve will develop a heart of sacrificial love.

TRAINING YOUR TEAM FOR KEY MISSIONS

Once your Bible Talk begins to function as a cohesive team, you can train them to excel in specific missions such as:

1. **Making disciples**
2. **Raising funds for special church projects**
3. **Serving the poor and needy**

Training Sessions: Dedicate time during your weekly Bible Talk meetings or discipling groups to train your team. Share lessons, teach practical skills, and review how the group is progressing toward its goals.

Role Playing: Practice real-life scenarios, such as sharing faith, leading a Bible study, or answering questions during a discussion. Role-playing builds confidence and helps members develop essential skills.

Feedback: After any team activity, provide constructive feedback. Celebrate what went well, and offer suggestions for improvement. Immediate feedback reinforces learning and encourages growth.

Praise and Celebrate: Nothing motivates people like recognition and celebration. Highlight individual and group achievements, and express your appreciation for their efforts.

CONCLUSION

Jesus understood the power of teamwork. Even though He could have accomplished His mission alone, He chose to build a team—a group of ordinary people who would accomplish extraordinary things together.

In the same way, you can lead your Bible Talk to become a united and effective team. By creating opportunities to grow together, assigning roles that align with each member's strengths, and committing to consistent improvement, you'll build a group that reflects God's love and purpose.

As your team grows closer and more effective, you'll see lives transformed, faith deepened, and God's mission fulfilled—one soul at a time.

Chapter 14

The Power of Daily Ministry

His speech persuaded them. They called the apostles in and had them flogged. Then they ordered them not to speak in the name of Jesus, and let them go.

The apostles left the Sanhedrin, rejoicing because they had been counted worthy of suffering disgrace for the Name. Day after day, in the temple courts and from house to house, they never stopped teaching and proclaiming the good news that Jesus is the Messiah.

—Acts 5:40-42

Imagine for a moment being stripped of your clothes, then strung up to face punishment. And it was all because you deci-ded to stand up to the authorities, like Jesus did, and continue to preach in spite of the opposition.

The first lash stings like nothing you ever felt before. Then the second comes, and then the third. You look over at your partner and share a glance to say that, though this hurts, this is what we signed up for. And a smile comes across both of your faces as you realize that you are honoring your Lord by going through the same sufferings as he did. And you find strength knowing that this whipping with a common whip was no way compared to being flogged with the flagellum the Romans used.

After lash ten, you start to smile, making your tormentors even angrier. After lash fifteen, you start to sing in unison, as your tormentors pause, and you see the perplexed looks on their faces. Then you go through lash twenty, then thirty, then lash thirty-nine, and to your surprise it stops—because you were ready to take on thirty-nine more for your Lord.

Then you slump on the ground, holding your brother in arms, and picking each other up, you look with defiance at your tormentors, sending them a glance that says there is no way in hell you will ever stop preaching.

Your tormentors, though utterly perplexed, still command you to stop preaching in his name, and they think they won't ever have to worry about you after that beating.

A few days later, your tormentors meet to congratulate themselves for stomping out this Jesus infection that is spreading throughout Jerusalem like a virus. Because, they think, by chopping off the head of the snake, the leaders, the rest of the movement will die.

Then one person rushes in, and then another, and then a third saying the same thing. "The men you flogged and commanded to stop preaching, ever since you flogged them, they have been going out day after day, and from house to house preaching in the name of the Lord Jesus!"

And you can imagine their tormentors slumping in their chairs, with the realization of Gamaliel's words, "If this movement is from God, you will not be able to stop these men; you will only find yourselves fighting against God."

If you were one of the apostles, how would you have responded after being flogged thirty-nine times and commanded not to speak in his name? Would you have taken a long-needed break? Would you have felt justified waiting for your wounds to heal to get back out to work? Would you have delegated the work of the ministry to someone else? Or would you have cowered under the pressure and threat of the authorities?

Then why did the apostles not do any of these things, but instead, they went out day after day, and from house to house proclaiming that Jesus is Lord?

Because, in Acts 4:13 it says:

> *When they saw the courage of Peter and John and realized that they were unschooled, ordinary men, they were astonished and they took note that these men had been with Jesus.*

These men had caught the heart of the Lord of Lords and the King of Kings. And that heart was the heart and love of daily ministry.

THE POWER OF DAILY MINISTRY

"In that hour Jesus said to the crowd, 'Am I leading a rebellion, that you have come out with swords and clubs to capture me? Every day I sat in the temple courts teaching, and you did not arrest me.'"

—Matthew 26:55

Jesus' ministry was a daily commitment. Every day, He taught, healed, served, and trained those around Him, demonstrating what it looks like to live fully for God. His disciples followed His example, taking up their crosses daily and dedicating themselves to God's work.

The early church carried on this daily devotion:

"Every day they continued to meet together in the temple courts. They broke bread in their homes and ate together with glad and sincere hearts, praising God and enjoying the favor of all the people. And the Lord added to their number daily those who were being saved."

—Acts 2:46-47

They didn't wait for special occasions or scheduled events to live out their faith. They lived it daily. They worshipped, shared, encouraged, and served every single day. This daily commitment created a powerful movement that changed the world—and it's a model for us to follow today.

WHAT IS DAILY MINISTRY?

Daily ministry is about doing the small, consistent things that reflect God's love and advance His kingdom. It's not about grand gestures or extraordinary events; it's about the steady, faithful actions we take every day:

1. **Daily Worship and Prayer**
    Spend time with God every morning, reading His Word and praying for guidance, strength, and opportunities to serve.

2. **Daily Openness**
    Be honest about your struggles, temptations, and victories. Share your heart with trusted brothers and sisters, and help them do the same.

3. **Daily Sharing of Faith**
    Look for opportunities to share the gospel—whether it's inviting someone to Bible Talk, starting a spiritual conversation, or offering to pray for someone.

4. **Daily Discipleship**
    Invest in the spiritual growth of others. Encourage your fellow disciples, help the weak, and disciple with love and truth.

5.   **Daily Bible Study**
     Teach non-believers through Bible studies, moving their hearts closer to making Jesus Lord.

A DISCIPLE'S MODEL WEEK

What does daily ministry look like in practice? Imagine Jesus taking over your life for a week. Would He spend hours scrolling through social media or binge-watching shows? Probably not. Instead, He would be sharing His faith, serving others, and making time for worship every single day.

Even with a busy schedule, daily ministry is possible. It's about incorporating small, meaningful actions into your routine like:

- Praying during your commute.
- Sharing your faith on lunch breaks.
- Encouraging someone with a quick phone call or text.
- Using evenings for Bible studies or fellowship.

WHY DAILY MINISTRY MATTERS

Daily ministry creates momentum. When every day is filled with worship, sharing, and serving, God's power is unleashed. The early church grew daily because they lived daily for God.

If your Bible Talk isn't growing, it may be because daily ministry hasn't become your standard. Weekly events and occasional outreach are good, but they don't compare to the impact of daily devotion.

HOW TO START DAILY MINISTRY IN YOUR BIBLE TALK

To create a culture of daily ministry, start by focusing on these areas:

1. **Set the Example**
   As a leader, demonstrate daily ministry in your own life. Share your experiences and inspire your group to follow your lead.

2. **Encourage Daily Worship**
   Challenge your Bible Talk members to have consistent quiet times, praying and studying God's Word every morning.

3. **Promote Daily Sharing**
   Encourage each member to make new friends daily. Celebrate their efforts and successes at Bible Talk meetings.

4. **Organize Daily Opportunities**
   Schedule consistent activities like prayer walks, outreach events, or service projects. Provide opportunities for members to work together in ministry.

5. **Build a Culture of Encouragement**
   Encourage your group to support and disciple each other daily. Use texts, calls, and in-person meetings to keep the group connected and inspired.

THE RESULTS OF DAILY MINISTRY

The apostles never stopped proclaiming Jesus, even after facing persecution. Their daily ministry built the foundation of the church and brought countless people to salvation. When we embrace daily ministry, we carry on that legacy.

> *"And the Lord added to their number daily those who were being saved."*
>
> **—Acts 2:47**

When your Bible Talk commits to daily ministry, you'll see God do amazing things. Lives will change, hearts will be transformed, and people will come to know Jesus.

CONCLUSION

Daily ministry isn't just for the apostles or the early church—it's for all of us. It's the consistent, faithful actions we take every day that create lasting impact.

Let's make the decision to live for Jesus daily. Let's pray, share, serve, and encourage every day. When we do, we'll experience the same power and growth that the early church did.

The power of daily ministry is real, and it's available to anyone willing to live it. Let's commit to being disciples who follow Jesus every day—and let's watch as God works miracles through our faithfulness.

Conclusion

Being a leader who helps people grow closer to God is one of the greatest callings we could ever embrace. It's not always easy, but it's profoundly rewarding because we're not just building a group or fulfilling a task—we're building God's family here on Earth.

This family isn't just a collection of individuals; it's a sanctuary of love, support, and closeness to God. Like the early church in Acts 2:42-47, we are striving to create a community where people are devoted to prayer, fellowship, sharing, and serving. It's a place where hearts are transformed, relationships are strengthened, and lives are changed.

God's promise to add to our numbers still holds true today. When we follow the timeless model of the early church—meeting together, teaching the Word, sharing in prayer, and caring for one another—we align ourselves with God's design for His people. And when God sees this kind of unity and devotion, He blesses it abundantly by drawing more souls into His Kingdom.

This isn't about building the largest or most impressive group; it's about cultivating a community that is deeply rooted in faith, love, and obedience to God. Even the smallest groups, when filled with devoted hearts, can make an eternal impact.

The beauty of this work is that it's accessible to everyone. You don't need to have all the answers or be flawless in your faith. God isn't looking for perfection; He's looking for people who are willing to love Him, love others, and take small but faithful steps toward His purpose.

It begins with simple, consistent habits—daily prayer, reading the Bible, and reaching out to those around you. From these small steps, a ripple effect of growth and transformation emerges. As leaders, our role is to set the tone, lead by example, and guide others with encouragement and grace. We help people stay focused on God, lift them up when they stumble, and celebrate their victories along the way.

What's amazing about this journey is how it transforms us as well. By pouring into others, we grow deeper in our faith, stronger in our trust in God, and more purposeful in our lives. We become a beacon of light, showing others what it means to follow Jesus in the midst of everyday life.

Whether you're starting with a few people gathered in a living room or leading a thriving Bible Talk, remember that every effort matters. Each prayer offered, each conversation about God, and each act of love builds up His Kingdom. And as we remain faithful in these small, consistent acts, God will continue to bless our efforts, just as He did in the days of the apostles.

So keep going. Keep loving. Keep building. God is with you every step of the way, empowering you to make an eternal difference. Together, we can fulfill His vision of a worldwide family united by faith, hope, and love.

The time is now, and God is ready to work through you. Let's rise to the challenge, and build God's Kingdom one Bible Talk at a time, and watch as God does incredible things in and through our lives.

And to God be the glory!

Amen.

Appendix

12 Bible Talk Lessons for the New Bible Talk Leader

Here are some effective bible discussions that are: Fun, Engaging, Entertaining, and Deeply Convicting (FEED) that you can use to practice with in your Bible Talk.

Feel free to remove or add parts to the lesson to make it work for your BT. Modify it to your speaking style. And, feel free to add your own personal stories, examples, illustrations, etc.

Review and study out the Bible Talk at least once before presenting the Bible Talk. Don't just pick one and use it 5 minutes before Bible Talk.

Tips for Presenting the Bible Talk

1. Make the Bible Talk 30-45 min max.
2. Be dynamic in your speaking (alternate between soft, authoritative, funny, etc. to keep it interesting).

3. Have some prepared answers for questions in case no one answers.
4. Make the BT fun, entertaining, and most importantly, convicting.
5. Choose only 3-4 people maximum to answer each question.
6. Say "great answer" when people answer to motivate them to answer more.
7. Rely on God (scriptures), and your BT (disciples) to do most of the heavy lifting.
8. Shorter is better, because it leaves them wanting more (and motivates them to want to study the Bible).
9. Keep it simple and avoid going on tangents.
10. Remember the Bible Talk is 50% for visitors, and 50% for Christians.

Abbreviations:

- Q—Question
- P—Point
- T—Transition
- RQ—Rhetorical Question or One answer question.
- M—Metaphor

Bible Discussion 1: Building Your House on the Rock

Q: If you had a magic wand and could build any amazing house you wanted, what house would you create?

Q: What if you found out later you accidentally built your house on a major earthquake fault line—How would you feel whenever an earthquake hit?

Q: If you wanted to make sure your beautiful house would last a long time what would you do before you built it?

Title—Build Your House on the Rock

Matthew 7:24-27

Building on the Rock

Q: Why do you think Jesus compared obeying God like building your house on a rock?

Q: What kind of storms do we face in our lives that puts our house to the test?

Q: Why does God promise that obeying him will allow you to withstand any storm in your life?

Q: Why isn't it enough just to obey a little?

P: If we follow God we can be guaranteed that we will build the best life possible, and even during the storms, we will stand.

Building on Sand

Q: What would happen to your beautiful house if you built it on sand?

Q: Why does Jesus compare not following God to building your house on sand?

Q: How do you feel when the storms come into your life, and you have no security or nothing firm to rely on?

Q: Ultimately, what do you think would be the greatest crash in our lives if we don't obey God?

P: If we don't obey God when the storms come, we won't have anything to rely on.

P2: Worse, if we don't obey God, our house will fall with a great crash after we die.

Story or Video (optional)—The Big China Crash

Recap

- If we follow God, we can be guaranteed we will build the best life possible, and even during the storms, it will stand.
- But if we don't obey God, when the storms come we won't have anything to rely on.
- Worse, ultimately, if we don't follow God, our house will fall with a great crash after we die.
- But if we obey God, not only can we live a great life here, but we will be able to live a great life for eternity.

Decision

RQ: If you're going to build a beautiful house, do you want it to stand or fall?

D: Then you need to decide today to fully obey God and his word.

Because only then will you truly build your house on the Rock.

Thanks for coming
So glad you could join us

Story—The Big China Crash

The biggest collapse in history due to bad construction, which also killed the most people, is the 1976 Tangshan earthquake in China. Although the earthquake was a natural disaster, the massive loss of life was largely attributed to poor construction practices and the failure to adhere to building standards in the rapidly expanding industrial city of Tangshan.

On July 28, 1976, a 7.5 magnitude earthquake struck Tangshan, a city of about one million people. The collapse of poorly constructed buildings and infrastructure led to one of the deadliest earthquakes in recorded history. Estimates of the death toll vary widely, but it is generally believed that between 242,000 and 655,000 people were killed.

The scale of the disaster was exacerbated by the fact that many of the buildings in Tangshan were not designed to withstand such a powerful earthquake. The city's rapid industrialization in the years leading up to the earthquake led to a boom in construction, but safety and quality were often sacrificed in favor of speed and cost-saving measures. As a result, many buildings, including residential apartments, factories, and public structures, collapsed almost immediately when the earthquake struck.

This disaster is a tragic example of how poor construction practices, combined with a lack of adherence to building codes and standards, can lead to catastrophic consequences in the event of a natural disaster.

Bible Discussion 2: The Parable of the Sower

Q: What is one of your favorite hobbies and why?

Q: If Jesus had a hobby, what do you think it would be?

I think it would be gardening.

Because most of his parables were about farmers. (Just kidding)

Let's look at one of Jesus's parables that described how he saw the whole world.

Title—Where Will You Be for Eternity?

Read Mark 4: 1-8

Q: What's going on here?

Q: What is a parable?

  ○ A parable is a metaphor to help us understand God's messages better.

Q: Why is it that sometimes Jesus used stories to share God's word with us?

First Seed

Q: What happened to the First seed that fell On the path?

Q: Why is it that the birds came and ate it up so quickly?

Second Seed

Q: What happened to the second seed that fell on the rocky places?

Q: Why is it that on rocky places, it could not have roots?

  ○ Usually with rocky soil, there is a layer of rocks or even bedrock under the soil and the roots cannot penetrate and get deep.

Third Seed

Q: What happened to the third seed that fell among the thorns?
Q: Why is it that the thorns choked the plants?
- When seed grows among thorns, the thorns suck up all of the moisture and nutrients so that the plant does not get what it needs to grow to maturity and bear fruit.

Fourth Seed

Q: What happened to the fourth seed that fell on the good soil?
Q: How is it that the seed on Good soil was able to produce such a big crop?
- The soil produces fruit, and the fruit produces seeds that produce more fruit, and so on.

Let's look at the interpretation of the parable:

Read Mark 4:13-20

Q: First of all, to whom does this parable apply?
Q: Jesus says the seed is the word of God—How is the word of God like a seed?

The Hard Heart

Q: What did Jesus say that the seed sown on the path represented?
Q: What are some ways that Satan tries to snatch the word away from us on a constant basis?
P: So if this is you, Jesus would say you have a Hard Heart

The Shallow Heart

Q: What did Jesus say that the seed sown on the rocky soil represented?

Q: What are some things that we can do to develop deep roots and not fall away?

P: If this is you, Jesus would say you have a Shallow Heart

The Strangled Heart

Q: What did Jesus say that the seed sown in thorny places represented?

Q: How does the worries of life, deceitfulness of wealth and desires for other things choke out God's word from our life?

Q: How do you know when you are the third seed?
  o When you stop being fruitful.

Q: What can we do to prevent these distractions from preventing us from being fruitful?

P: If this is you, Jesus would say you have a Strangled Heart

The Humble/Fruitful Heart

Q: What did Jesus say that the seed sown in the Good soil represented?

Q: What do you think he means by producing a crop?

Q: If you are not making an effort to produce a crop, then what does this mean?

Q: How do we make sure that we become the last seed and not any of the first 3?
  o He said we need to hear the word and accept it.
  o He said we need to make an effort to produce a crop.

P: If this is you, Jesus would say you have a Humble, fruitful Heart

Recap

The interesting thing is that there will be a harvest time when God (the farmer) is going to harvest all of his fruit.

He's only going to harvest the good fruit, and all the rest will be crushed.

So Jesus is giving us plenty of time to prepare before it's too late.

But only one of the soils is the one that pleased God.

The question is, which one are you?

- If you're not reading your Bible, you're the hardened heart.
- If you're emotionally up and down, you're the shallow heart
- If you're worried and distracted, you're the strangled heart.

The Good news is that if you are one of the first three seeds, you have time to change!

- And you can grow in your passion and zeal for God and become the humble and fruitful heart.

Decision

So the question is, after today, which heart will you decide to be?

- Because it will determine where you will be—for eternity.

~~~~~~~~~~~~

Thanks for coming.
So glad you could make it.

Bible Discussion 3: The Rich Young Ruler

Q: What is one thing that if you just had more of, your life would be so much better?

Q: What are ways it would make your life better?

Q: What do you think God thinks is the one thing, that if you had more of it, your life would be so much better?

P: Isn't it amazing how what God thinks we need is so different from what we think we need?

Today, we're going to look at a man who had to wrestle with One Big Thing in His Life and what God thought about it.

Title—The One Big Thing

Mark 10:17-22

Q: How would you describe this guy?

Q: Why was all his religiosity and goodness not enough to save him?

Q: Why was One thing such a big deal to God? I mean it was just one thing!

Q: Why would this intelligent, religious guy let this One Thing keep him from making it to heaven?

RQ: Was this one thing worth losing his salvation for and going to hell for eternity?

○ No

Many of us are religious, like this guy.

RQ: Makes you wonder, what one thing is preventing us from being wholehearted about God?

○ Maybe it's a sin we aren't ready to give up yet

○ Maybe it's a relationship we're not ready to give up for God.

○ Maybe it's what we know we need to do, but we just are not ready to start doing it for God.

○ Or maybe it's the commitment to be wholehearted for God.

Q: What are ways that our One Big Thing sometimes gets in your way of being totally devoted to God?

Q: RQ: Are the things we cling to going to bring us what we desperately want?

- o No

Q: Why not?

RQ: Then, is this thing really worth jeopardizing your eternal life for?

- o No

Video or Story (Choose one): The Lady and the Train

Q: What did you think about that (story)?

Q: Ultimately, Why did this very intelligent, successful and religious young man not follow Jesus and make it to heaven?

- o Because he wasn't willing to give up on his One Big Thing

Recap

THINK ABOUT YOUR ONE BIG THING

RQ: After everything we looked at today, is it really worth jeopardizing or sacrificing your relationship with God for?

Decision

RQ: Then are you ready to give up this ONE BIG THING and Make God Your One Big Thing?

Q: WHEN? Now!!!

Then let's make a decision to let go of our One Big Thing Today so that God will truly become our ONE BIG THING!

~~~~~~~~

Thanks for Coming
So Glad you could join us.

Story—The Lady and The Train

News Article Circa NYC – 1990's

A horrifying event transpired today involving a commuter's death on a train station platform when the strap of her expensive handbag became lodged between the train's doors.

The 57-year-old woman was reported running for the train and slamming into the doors.

Realizing that she had just missed the train, she admitted defeat and calmly started to walk away from the train.

But it wasn't until the train started to move away from the platform that the woman noticed her expensive handbag had become lodged in the doors.

Instead of letting the bag go, the woman holds on to it for dear life, following it along the platform.

Commuters waiting on the platform looked on in dismay, shouting at the woman to let the bag go.

"Let it go!" they yelled.

"It's not worth it!" They continued.

"It's only a handbag!" Someone else yelled.

"It's not worth your life!" A voice is heard in the background.

Then the woman could be seen running to keep up with the train for just a few steps.

Then the next thing, the horrified onlookers reported, is that the train began to accelerate, but the lady just couldn't keep up.

Then as the onlookers horrifically watched, she was sucked in between the platform and the subway car and ultimately underneath onto the tracks.

Then the woman was dragged in between the subway cars, and ultimately fatally run over by the train.

The crowd of people just stood there in silence, dumbfounded...

They just tried to make sense of what just happened, and to understand why the woman wouldn't just let go of her bag and save her own life.

"It was just a bag," a traumatized onlooker was reported repeating over and over.

"It was just a bag..."

"It was just a bag..."

Bible Discussion 4: The Parable of the Hidden Treasure

(It's Going to Cost You Everything)

Q: When was a situation where you scored a really great deal, and how did you feel? (Discount, Opportunity, etc).

Q: Why are we so happy when we find a great deal?

Transition—Let's look at a couple of guys in the Bible who stumbled across a really great deal, and how they felt about it.

Title—It's Going to Cost Everything

Matt 13:44

Q: Why do you think Jesus compares the Kingdom of Heaven to a treasure?

Q: Why do you think Jesus says that the treasure is hidden?

Q: Why would this person be willing to sell everything they have to get this treasure?

Matt 13:45

This time, it's a merchant looking for fine pearls—

Q: How have we searched long and hard for God in our lives before we were Christians?

The Bible says the pearl is the kingdom of heaven.

Q: What makes the kingdom of heaven so valuable that these guys would sell everything they had to get it?

Q: How do you think these guys felt when they got their treasure?

Q: So what do you think is the point of Jesus's parable?

RQ: When Jesus said to give up everything—is Jesus saying we need to sell all of our stuff and go out into the street and hold a big sign saying the End is Near?

　　○ No

But it's like this:

Story—The Pearl of Great Price

RQ: Who do you think the old man in the story is?
- o God

Q: What do you think the pearl is?
- o The Kingdom of God.

Q: And if you want it, how much is it going to cost you?
- o It's going to cost you everything!

Q: So then, what does a person's life look like that has surrendered everything to God?

Recap

- Jesus is trying to tell us that the Kingdom of Heaven is very valuable.
- But if you want it, it's going to cost you everything that you have.
- Giving up everything means that everything you have will be used for God's purpose now.

Decision

So you need to ask yourself, do I want to be part of the Kingdom of God?

Well, if you want it, what's it going to cost?
- It's going to cost everything.

So, are you ready to surrender everything to God?

The choice is yours to make.

Thanks for coming
So glad you could make it.

Story—The Pearl of Great Price

Suppose you were a merchant of fine pearls. And you heard of a legendary pearl of great price.

Now as a collector of fine pearls you decided to dedicate your life looking for this pearl.

Imagine that you searched for many years, and finally, a foreigner comes to visit your shop and he brings you the pearl of great price for you to see.

Immediately you say, "I must have this pearl—name your price and I will pay it!"

The gentleman says, "I am sorry, this pearl has been in my family for generations, and is not for sale."

But you beg and plead with him—"You don't understand, I have been looking for this pearl all my life—I need to have it, I will give you everything that I have!"

"Everything you have, huh?"

"Yes, everything I have."

The man says, "OK, but it is going to cost you everything you have."

So you gleefully sign the contract agreeing to buy the pearl for everything that you have. You pull out your check book, and you make him out a check for $10 Million dollars on the spot.

The man takes the check, and then looks at you and asks, "What about your wallet. I said everything you have."

"My wallet? Well it is a $500 dollar wallet, but hey, it's worth it." So you give him your wallet.

"Hey can I have my driver's license so I can get back home?" You say.

He says, "You have a car? That's mine too. I said everything you have."

"My car! Oh man." You say out loud. "But, how am I supposed to get back home?"

"You have a house?" he says. "That's mine too; I said everything that you have."

"My house! Wow, what am I going to tell my wife and kids?!"

"You have a wife and kids?" They're mine too. I said everything you have."

"My wife and kids! Oh my gosh, what have I done?"

And as you're contemplating the fact that you just gave up everything, he looks at you and says...

"You know what? You're mine too. I said everything you have."

Then he takes out the pearl and gives it to you. You are so very happy, but sad as well, because you just realize you gave up everything you own and sold yourself and your family to slavery.

Then he looks at you and starts to laugh, "Ha ha ha ha..." Then he says, "You know what? I don't need all your stuff, I'm filthy rich. And I have plenty of pearls. But here is what I will do.

Here's your check, I am going to give you your money back—but don't forget now you need to use that money the way I want you to use it, because that is now my money.

And, here's your car and house back—but now you need to drive who I want you to drive around, and let who I want you to let stay at that house, because that is my car and my house now.

Here are your wife and kids back—but remember now you need to treat that wife the way I want you treat her, and raise those kids the way I want you to raise them, because don't forget that is my wife and those are my kids.

And here's your life back. But now you need to live the way I want you to live, because don't forget; now you're mine."

Bible Discussion 5: The Wedding Banquet

Q: What was the last great party you attended, and what made it so much fun?

Q: What were some things you had to do to prepare for the party?

Q: If God were throwing a party, how amazing would it be?

How would you like to be invited to a party God is throwing?

Title—A Party Like No Other

Matt 22:1-7

Q: Who wants to give a summary of what happened?

Q: If a great king is throwing this banquet, what kind of banquet do you think it would be?

Q: How would you feel if you prepared an excellent banquet for your son or daughter and the people you invited refused to come?

Q: Why do you think he kept asking people to come to his banquet?

Q: Why would someone refuse to come to such a great banquet?

Matt 22: 8-10

Q: Why do you think he went to this extent to bring people into his banquet?

Metaphor—
- Imagine you threw a banquet for your 8-year-old, and nobody came.
- Q: What would you do?

Matt 22: 11-14

Background
- It says that the man wasn't wearing the right clothes and was thrown out.
- You see, in Jesus' time, usually when you were invited to a party, you were given clothes to wear.

Q: So, why wouldn't this person wear the clothes he was given?
Q: What do you think Jesus meant by: "many are invited, but few are chosen?"
T: What do you think the clothes are that he is expecting us to wear?

Galatians 3: 26-27

Q: What do you think he means by clothing yourself with Jesus Christ?
RQ: If you're not wearing the clothes God has prepared for you, then whose clothes are you wearing?
Q: What kind of clothes does Satan have prepared for you?
- Slave clothes
- Shackles
- Dog Collar with shocks
Q: What will it take to make sure we put on God's clothes and not Satan's clothes?

Recap

- The Bible says, Many are called, but few are chosen.
- But it's all based on the clothes you wear.
- So when he calls, we need to make sure that we are wearing the right clothes.

Decision

Well, if you are here, then God has definitely invited you to his banquet.
- But you need to have the right clothes to get in.

The question is, are you ready to put on the right clothes today?
- If you are, then make a decision to study the bible and be like Jesus.

Then, we can all truly take part in A Party Like No Other, both now and in heaven.

Bible Discussion 6: The Parable of the Bags of Gold

Q: When was a situation where you worked really hard for something and you finally got it?

Q: How did you feel finally accomplishing your goal?

Q: Why does it bother us so much when we see lazy people who feel entitled to something that they never worked for?

10 Signs You Are Lazy

If you've lived by any of these, then you are lazy.

1. The farther away the remote is, the more you like what's already on TV
2. If something falls under the bed, it's gone forever.
3. If you spill water, it will eventually dry.
4. Don't charge your phone until it says 1% remaining.
5. Forget the Terms and Conditions, just hit Accept
6. If it's not on the first page of Google, it doesn't exist
7. Why make your bed when you're just going to get back in it again?
8. If you're late, don't go.
9. If you drop the ice cube, just kick it under the fridge.
10. If I can't reach it, then I don't need it.

Today we're going to look at a few guys that were given a chance to work hard to earn some great rewards and how it turned out.

Title—Are You Faithful or Are You Lazy?

Matt 25:14 -15

Q: Who do you think the Master is in this story?
   ○ God

Q: And who are the servants?
   ○ We are—his disciples.

Q: What do you think the valuable property is, that he entrusted to us, his servants?

Q: What do you think the bags of gold represent?
   o The Gospel
   o The knowledge of Salvation
   o His Word

P: So God has entrusted you with something incredibly valuable (his word/gospel), and now he expects you to do something with it.

Matthew 25:16-18

Q: What happens in the story here?

First 2 Servants

Q: What are some things you think they had to do in order to grow their masters' money?

Q: What are some characteristics you think they needed to have in order to double their Master's money?

Q: What do you think motivated them to work so hard (they were only slaves!)?

Q: What are some things that we need to do in order to multiply what God has given us and bring more to our Master?

RQ: Does this describe you?

The Lazy Servant

Q: What do you think would compel the last servant to dig a hole and hide his Master's money?

Q: What do you think went through the Lazy servant's mind as he saw how hard the other two servants were working?

T: Let's see what happens next:

Matthew 25:19-23

Q: Why do you think the servants were so happy to tell the Master what they had done for him?

Q: Why do you think the Master responded the way he did?

Q: What do you think goes through God's mind when he sees us working hard: sharing our faith, studying the Bible with people and baptizing people day after day?

T: Let's see what happened to the other servant...

Matthew 25:24-30

Q: How did the servant with the one bag of gold respond to the Master?

Q: Why do you think the Master called this servant wicked and lazy for not growing his money?
   o Fearful = selfish (wicked)
   o Lazy = unwilling

Q: What are ways that our selfishness and laziness prevent us from working hard for God?

Story or Video (optional)

Recap

- The first two servants were:
   o Hard-working
   o Diligent
   o Motivated by the desire to please the master
   o Worked hard day after day in order to grow what the Master entrusted to them.

- The lazy servant was
   o Selfish
   o Lazy

- Put his happiness over the Master's happiness
- Gained nothing for the Master
- And was ultimately cast out

Q: What was the biggest difference between the hearts of the Hardworking Servants and the Lazy servant?

P: The hard-working servants made the Master's happiness more important than their own.
   - The lazy servant put his happiness over the Master's.

Look at your life

- RQ: Which one describes you?
- RQ: Are you going out day after day, diligently working hard to grow what God has entrusted to you?
- RQ: Are you using your gifts to save more souls and ultimately make the Master happy?
- RQ: Or, have you just buried the gospel and spent most of your time focused on taking care of yourself?

Decision

The moral—This is a parable about judgment day.

- And it's saying: if you're selfish and lazy, and don't pour yourself out for the master's business—then you're not going to make it.
- But if you make the master's happiness more important than your own...
   - By sharing your faith and studying the Bible with people, day after day. to save souls...
- Not only will you save many people and bring more souls to the Master...
- But you'll be able to ultimately share in your Master's happiness.

So, what kind of servant will you be?

- The Lazy servant?
- A Faithful servant?

But only one can share in the Master's happiness.

The choice is up to you.

~~~~~~~~~~~~~~~~~~

Thank for coming
So glad you could make it

Bible Discussion 7: Jesus Walks on Water

Q: What are some common things that distract us in life?
Q: When was a time you got distracted and things did not go very well?
Q: Why do we get distracted so easily?

Distraction—when you choose to focus on things that aren't important, and it causes you to neglect things that are most important.

Title—Fix Your Eyes on Jesus

Matt 14:22-25

Q: What's going on here?
Q: What were the signs that prayer was something important to Jesus?
Q: Even though Jesus was really busy, why did Jesus spend so much time in prayer?
Q: How differently would your life look like if you had a prayer life like Jesus?

Matt 14: 25-29

Q: How would you feel if you were in the middle of the sea, in total darkness, and then you saw somebody just walking by?
Q: Why do you think this was so terrifying for the disciples?
Q: What do you think made Peter ask Jesus to help him walk on water?
Q: Why is it that when you are close to God, you feel like you can do anything (and miracles are possible)?
Q: Why do you think Jesus granted Peter's wish?
Q: What are some miracles God has done in your life as a disciple?
T: The story could've just ended there. But let's see what happened.

Matt 14:30-33

Q: Peter was doing so well, so what caused Peter to doubt (and ultimately sink)?
   Satan doesn't want us to walk on water.

Q: What are some things that Satan uses to distract us and take our eyes off of Jesus?

Q: What can we do to prevent ourselves from getting distracted and help us keep our eyes on God and Jesus daily?

Recap

- Even though he was scared, Peter walked on the water!
- But because he got distracted and took his eyes off of Jesus, he began to sink.
- Like Peter, God wants to do great miracles in our lives.
- But that means we've got to do everything possible to Fix our eyes on Jesus.

Decision

RQ: Are you going to let Satan use distractions to keep you from seeing miracles?

Then it's time to throw off all the distractions and whatever sin is entangling you—and fix your eyes on Jesus.

And before you know it, you'll be walking on water.

Thanks for coming
So glad you could make it.

Bible Discussion 8: Jesus Calms the Storm

Optional: Trust Exercise Video: epic trust fall.exe

Q: Who is someone you trust most in your life and why?
Q: What does the word trust mean to you?
Q: Why is trust so important to really make a relationship work?

Title—Trusting God During Tough Times

Mark 4:35-36

Q: What's going on here?
Q: How tired do you think Jesus was from healing and helping the crowds of people before this?

Mark 4:37

Q: What happens here?
Q: How do you think these disciples felt being in this kind of storm?
Q: What are some situations we go through in life that make you feel so bad that you feel like you are going through a really bad storm?

Mark 4:38

Q: How would you feel if you were going through a life-threatening storm, and there was Jesus taking a nap through the whole thing?

Metaphor—
Q: How would you feel if you're in an airplane in free fall, and you look through the cockpit door, and the pilot is sleeping on a cushion?
Q: When we go through tough times, and we don't see God helping us, what do we sometimes feel?
Q: With all the craziness going on, why do you think Jesus slept through it?

Q: But, what are some reasons that when we go through storms, God doesn't do anything about it right away?

Q: And when we don't see God do things right away, how do we sometimes respond?

T: The disciples were feeling the same things. Let's see what happens:

Mark 4: 39—40

Q: What happens here?

Q: If Jesus has the power to rebuke the wind and the waves, then how powerful is he?

Q: Why do you think he rebuked his disciples?
- Their fear revealed their lack of faith.

P: Your level of fear/worry/anxiety reveals your level of faith.
- It is a good indicator of how much we trust God.

Story or Video (Optional):

Recap

- God is all-powerful and can do anything.
- But sometimes, he allows us to go through storms to test us.
- And our fear or trust will reveal the level of our faith.
- But no matter how scary it is, God loves you and is powerful enough to get you through it.

Decision

The question is, when you are tested, are you going to give into your fear? Or are you going to have faith?

If you choose faith, then make a decision today that when the storms come, you will put away your fear and choose faith.

And show God you will trust him even during tough times.

And in his time, God will get you through it.

Thanks for coming.
So glad you could make it.

Bible Discussion 9: The Demon-Possessed Man

Q: How do you feel about meeting new people and why?

Q: What's a situation where you thought someone was one way, but when you got to know them, they were totally different from what you expected?

Q: How do you feel when people judge you without really getting to know you?

Let's look at a situation where Jesus met a guy that was totally different than he was—and what he did.

Title—Don't judge a book by its cover

Mark 5:1-5

Q: How does the Bible describe this man?

Q: How would most people treat a guy like this?

Mark 5: 6-8

Q: How would you feel if you were the disciples and you'd see this guy running full speed at you?

Q: But Jesus stands there—what would you be thinking about Jesus at this point?

Q: Then, what happens when he meets Jesus?

Q: Next thing, Jesus asks him his name—if you were one of the disciples, what would be going through your mind at this point?

Q: What was the real cause of all of this man's issues?

P: Jesus, I could see that this guy was more than what he was on the outside.

Q: How does it feel when people really take time to get to know who you really are, instead of judging you from the outside?

Q: What are some ways when we share our faith, to not get distracted by the outside—but really get to know what is going on in people's lives?

Mark 5: 11-17

Q: What happened here?

Q: Why do you think they responded this way to Jesus healing this man?

Q: Why is it that people are so afraid of change, even if the change is good for them?

Mark 5:18-20

Q: How do you think this man felt, all those years living in the tombs?

Jesus helped this man overcome impossible and difficult things in his life.

Q: What are some things that only Jesus can help us overcome in our lives?

Q: What do you think compelled this man to share his faith with so many people (Ten Cities)?

Guess what?

At one point in our lives, we've all been the crazy, demon-possessed man or woman.

And somebody was willing to look past all the outside to care about you and introduce Jesus to you.

Q: How does that make you feel?

Story or Video (Optional): African-American man convinces Klansmen to leave the KKK through friendship
https://youtu.be/PVVFx3issHg?si=m-_7Rxzjlo4gf4Qb

Q: What do you think about that video?

Recap

- Most people were scared of the demon-possessed man because they only saw him on the outside.
- Jesus looked past the outside and saw this man's heart.
- And because of it Jesus was able to heal him.
- We can be distracted from sharing our faith if we only look at the outside.
- But if we love people like Jesus, we will be able to help people overcome impossible difficulties in their lives.

So the question is, are you going to judge a book by its cover?

Or will you be like Jesus and help their hearts, regardless of what's on the outside?

Just remember what someone did for you.

Thanks for coming
So glad you could join us.

Bible Discussion 10: The Armor of God

Q: If there was a zombie apocalypse—what gear would you make sure you have on and why?

Q: And what are some things you would do to make sure you would survive?

Read: Things To Do To Survive a Zombie Apocalypse (From the Internet)

- Get a trampoline—zombies have a tough enough time walking, so they'll never catch you.
- Surround yourself with treadmills.
- Go to Costco and buy weapons in bulk.
- The first person who says Zombies aren't real, use them as a human shield.
- Zombies can't climb mountains, so go to the Poconos.

Let's look at some spiritual gear God prepared for us, and why we shouldn't be caught dead without them.

Title—Don't be caught with your pants down

Ephesians 6:10-12

The Bible says that there is a spiritual war (apocalypse) going on right now.

Q: If you could see the spiritual battle with your own eyes, what do you think it would look like?

Q: How does it make you feel to know that there is a spiritual battle going on around you?

Q: What is the purpose of the spiritual battle?
- It is a battle for your soul.

The Bible says the devil has schemes:

Q: Why do you think the devil is scheming to make you fall?

Q: What are some of the best schemes that Satan uses against people today?

Q: If Satan really wanted you to fall, what one thing do you think he could use against you that would have the best chance at taking you down?

Satan has succeeded in causing millions of people to fall for thousands of years.

Q: What are you going to do to make sure that Satan doesn't succeed in taking you down?

T: The good news is that God doesn't leave us defenseless—Let's look at the special weapons that God has given us that can protect us.

Eph 6:13-18

God has given us special armor that can protect us from the devil's attacks:

1. Belt of Truth

- The belt of truth buckled around your waist to hold everything together

Q: What are some ways that Satan prevents us from knowing or hearing the truth?

2. Breastplate of righteousness-

- The breastplate of righteousness protects your heart.

Q: How does confessing and being open about our sins, temptations, and feelings protect your heart?

3. Feet Fitted with the Gospel of Peace

- Readiness to share the gospel

Q: How does sharing your faith protect your heart from Satan's attacks?

"It's really hard for Satan to hit a moving target."

4. Shield of Faith

- The Shield Protects you from arrows.

Q: How does your faith protect you from the flaming arrows Satan attacks us with every day?

5. Helmet of Salvation

- The helmet of salvation protects your mind.

Q: How will thinking about our salvation protect our minds from these unrighteous thoughts?

6. The sword of the spirit

- The sword of the spirit is the word of God.

Q: What are ways that swinging the sword of the spirit (the Bible) helps us to prevent giving into Satan's schemes?

RQ: If the Bible is the strongest weapon God has given us to defend ourselves, how often should we be using it?
- Every day.

(Optional) Now let's get a glimpse of what we're up against:

Story or Video (Optional): The Arrows In The Words of Satan Kinetic Typography https://youtu.be/65Td29aVx70?si=QEZijt7qciZlcN4b

Q: What stuck out to you in this video?

Recap

- If you wanted to survive a Zombie apocalypse, you would prepare!
- But right now we are in an Apocalypse, the spiritual war for our souls.

- The good news is that God has given us the perfect gear to face the battle and be victorious.

He's given us the:

- Belt of truth
- Breastplate of righteousness
- Shield of faith
- Helmet of Salvation
- Sword of the spirit

The question is: Have you been wearing the gear God gave you?

RQ: If not, What do you think will happen to you if you try to go into battle without your armor on?
  - You won't make it.

Decision

> *"If you're not fighting in the battle, then you're already a casualty of the war.*

My question for you is—Are you ready to fight?

- By reading your Bible every day and hearing the truth.
- By Being Open about your temptations and sins with others.
- By focusing your mind on things in heaven
- By sharing your faith and teaching the gospel to as many people as possible!

Because only then, when the battle is over, you won't be caught with your pants down.

Thanks for coming.
So glad you could join us

Bible Discussion 11: Hot, Cold or Lukewarm

Q: What is your favorite food that you like served hot, and why?

Q: What is your favorite food that you like served cold, and why?

Q: How do you feel when you order hot food or cold food at a restaurant, and it arrives warm?

Ex:

○ Warm soup

○ Warm ice cream

RQ: Isn't it interesting how not a lot of people like warm food?

What's really interesting is that God feels the same way about our faith.

Title—Is Your Relationship with God Hot, Cold, or Lukewarm?

Revelations 3:14-16

Q: How would you feel if Jesus came to your house and said I know your deeds, and it was time for a Christian performance review?

Q: What would Jesus consider a person with a cold commitment to him?

Q: What would Jesus consider a person with a hot commitment to him?

○ Passionate relationship with God.

Q: Why was Jesus the best example of a man with a passionate commitment to God?

Q: What would Jesus consider a person with a lukewarm commitment

Q: What are some things that cause us to get lukewarm towards God?

Q: Why do you think Jesus would rather have a relationship that is hot or cold instead of a relationship with a lukewarm person?

Metaphor:

Q: If you got married and your spouse decided they were going to have a lukewarm commitment, how would you feel?

Q: What would you think that would be like?

Q: How long would you tolerate a relationship like that?

Q: What does Jesus say he will do to people who have a lukewarm commitment to him?

- He is going to spit you out of his mouth.
- To spit you out of his mouth means to vomit you out of his mouth.

Q: Why do you think Jesus feels so strongly about lukewarm people?

Q: What are some things we can do to prevent us from becoming Lukewarm in our relationship with God?

God is passionate!

And God wants passion!

Q: What are some things you can do to become more passionate in your relationship with God?

Story or Video (Optional):

Recap

- If you are Hot in your commitment to God right now—Then it's time to get hotter.
- If you are cold in your commitment to God right now—Well if you're here, there is still hope for you.
- But if you are lukewarm about your commitment to God right now, then it's time to repent!
  - Make a decision that you are going to give your whole heart and be passionate towards God.

Decision

God is passionate!

And God will only accept passion in return.

So, are you ready to be hot for God?

Or will you experience the hotness of hell?

Either way, you will get hot.

~~~~~~~~~~~

Thanks for coming
So glad you could join us.

Bible Discussion 12: This Too Shall Pass

Q: What is something you've gone through in your life that you thought was the end of the world—but now, looking back on it you realize how silly it was?

Q: What changed that now it doesn't seem like that big of a deal anymore?

Q: What are some things that seem really important to us, but from God's perspective God thinks are really, really silly?

Title—This Too Shall Pass

Luke 16:13-15

Q: What can you learn about God in this passage?

Q: What can you learn about people in this passage?

Q: What are some ways we show God we love other things more than him?

Q: What are some things that we can place a lot of value in but are detestable in God's sight?

Q: How does it feel to know that what you could be valuing in your life could be offensive to God?

Q: What will help you know whether your life is pleasing or offensive to God?

P: We need to be careful that what is important to us is not detestable to God.

James 4:13-17

Q: What are some ways that we make plans about what we will do today, tomorrow, or a year from now?

Q: If you were God, why would you consider the way people make plans to be so silly?

Q: Why does he compare your life to a mist?

God is not saying all planning is bad.

Q: But what planning is bad, to God?
  ○ The plans you make without considering God.
  ○ The plans you depend on more than God.
Q: What does it look like when you make plans, but you put God first in your planning?
P: We need to make sure our plans are God's plans.
T: Let's look at another scripture that shows what we think is important is—is different than what God thinks is important

1 John 2:15-17

Q: What are some ways that we can love the world?
Q: Why does the bible say that when we love the world, we cannot love God?
  ○ You can't serve two masters.

Metaphor:
Q: How would you feel if your spouse brought a new person into your house to share your marriage with?
Q: How long would you tolerate that?
  ○ God feels the same way about sharing you with the world.
  ○ God is a jealous God!
Q: Why do you think from God's perspective, loving the world is just stupid?
Q: (vs17) Consider something that you really love, or consider really important—How does it feel to know it will pass away?
Q: How does it feel to know that if you do it God's way, you will live forever?
RQ: Which sounds like a better deal to you?

Story or Video (Optional): The Ring

Recap

So imagine:
- Consider your education—This too shall pass
- Consider your career—This too shall pass.
- Consider your money—This too shall pass
- Consider your relationships—This too shall pass
- Consider your problems (money, relationships, physical)—This too shall pass.
- Consider your life—This too shall pass.

After your mist of a life disappears, and everything else disappears—the only thing that will remain is you, God and judgment day.

The question is, will God give you eternal life, or will God say about your life, "This too shall pass."

Decision

So, the question is:

Will you put your trust in what the world thinks is important?

Or will you put your hope in what God thinks is important?

But just remember, only one of them will pass away…and only one of them will live forever.

~~~~~~~~~~~~~~~~

Thanks for coming
So glad you could make it.

The Ring

Thousands of years ago, there was a wealthy king that decided to humble one of his most trusted ministers.

He said to him, "Benaiah,there is a certain ring that I want you to bring to me. I wish to wear it for the holiday of the Fall Harvest, which gives you six months to find it."

"If it exists anywhere on earth, your majesty," replied Benaiah, "I will find it and bring it to you. But what makes the ring so special?"

"It has magic powers," answered the king. "If a happy man looks at it, he becomes sad, and if a sad man looks at it, he becomes happy; and if a rich man looks at it, he becomes poor, but if a poor man looks at it, he becomes rich."

Now the king knew that no such ring existed in the world, but he wished to give his minister a little taste of humility.

Spring passed and then summer, and still Benaiah had no idea where he could find the ring.

On the night before the holiday of the Fall Harvest, he decided to take a walk in one of the poorest quarters of the kingdom.

He passed by an old merchant who had begun to set out the day's wares on a shabby carpet.

"Have you by any chance heard of a magic ring that makes the happy wearer forget his joy and the broken- hearted wearer forget his sorrows, and makes a rich man forget his riches, and a poor man forget his poverty?" asked Benaiah.

He watched the very old man take a plain wooden ring from his pocket and engrave something on it.

When Benaiah read the words on the ring, his face broke out in a wide smile.

Now, that night the entire city welcomed in the holiday of the Fall Harvest with great festivity.

"Well, my friend," said the wealthy King, "have you found what I sent you after?"

All the other ministers laughed and the wealthy King himself smiled.

Then, to everyone's surprise, Benaiah held up a small wooden ring and declared, "Here it is, your majesty!" And handed it to the king.

As soon as the King read the inscription, the smile immediately vanished from his face, and then a tear slowly fell down his cheek.

Then he passed it to the other ministers, and immediately all the smiles vanished from their faces also.

Then the rich King retired to his chambers in sorrow, as did all the other ministers.

Then Benaiah handed two of the King's slaves the wooden ring, as he returned to his chambers in sorrow as well.

And upon reading the ring's inscription, immediately a smile came to one of the servant's faces.

"What does it say?" the other servant pleaded. "What does it say?!!!"

"This too shall pass," he said with a smile.

"This too, shall pass."

www.ingramcontent.com/pod-product-compliance
Lightning Source LLC
Chambersburg PA
CBHW071753120626
46550CB00002B/776